THE MONROE DOCTRINE

Eng. by A.B.Durand. from the Painting by J.Vanderlyn in the City Hall New-York.

JAMES MONROE.

James Monroe

Portrait of James Monroe, engraving by A. B. Durand from the painting by J. Vanderlyn ca. 1820. Courtesy Kean Archives.

THE MONROE DOCTRINE

AN AMERICAN FRAME OF MIND

by

CHARLES MORROW WILSON

AUERBACH®
publishers

princeton
philadelphia
new york
london

Library of Congress Catalog Card Number: 78-147204
International Standard Book Number: 0-87769-069-3

First Printing

Printed in the United States of America

Contents

CONTENTS

List of Illustrations

PART I

THE MONROE DOCTRINE

1. The Name was James Monroe

ON THE SNOWY morning of December 2, 1823, a plainly dressed elderly man climbed carefully out of a large enclosed carriage and walked alone up the wide unpaved street to the stone-stepped entrance of the Capitol in Washington, D.C. He was rather tall, about five feet eleven, several inches above the then prevailing average, and his long stride showed a slight limp. He also was exceptionally broad shouldered and his knee-length gray cloak did not hide the fact that his right shoulder sagged noticeably. During the crucial revolutionary battle of Trenton in 1776 the shoulder had been torn apart by a British musket ball. The then-young lieutenant, formerly of the "Virginia Line," had never fully recovered from the wound.

At age sixty-five, the equivalent of a presentday eighty to eighty-five, he still showed the aftereffects of more than five years of extremely active and exceptionally widespread combat in the Revolution. He had survived a long list of important battles—at White Plains, Yonkers, Brandywine, Germantown, Monmouth—as well as Trenton and several more of what he described as "Mr. Washington's

13

early-morning river crossings." By his eighteenth year he had learned the hard way (beginning with his "White Plains fracas") that liberty is not always gained easily or painlessly.

Those who awaited his arrival in the big, arch-ceilinged hallway of the Capitol could have noted that the old man's head and alert gray-blue eyes and broad, high forehead were above average size. His thin-lipped saggy mouth had been described as enormous. His curly, neatly cropped hair was brownish red streaked with gray. His face, including his statuesque nose which many described as his best feature, was generously mottled with freckles.

Much of the time his face was expressionless. His wife Eliza explained in her Dutch accent (her family, the Kortwrights, were immigrant merchants from Amsterdam) that during his years of enduring pain from his battle wounds, her "gud hosban'" had developed an unusual passiveness. After all, the bodily pain he had suffered throughout much of his lifetime would have long since killed an ordinary man.

Eliza's husband was not an ordinary man. He was James Monroe, the fifth and, adjudged by vote count, the most popular president of the United States of America. In his reelection in 1820 he had carried every state of the Union and received all but one vote in the electoral college—for what remains an all-time record for presidential popularity. That provided further cause for his prevailing nickname, "Old Mr. America."

Even in his first presidential race in 1816, James Monroe had carried all but two of the then nineteen states, and despite a very able opponent (Rufus King of New York), his landslide victory had practically erased the long-dominant Federalist party. Yet, oddly enough,

Monroe had recently and ably served the party which he and his newly founded Republican-Democratic or "Common Peoples" party had so severely defeated.

All four of Mr. Monroe's White House predecessors had been distinguished although individualistic members of the American colonial aristocracy; at least during part of their lives all had been men of wealth as well as great prestige. But this fifth and most popular president was a man of the "common clay." Neither he nor his plain-living parents, Spence and Elizabeth Monroe, originally of rural Westmoreland County, Virginia, had ever pretended otherwise. Their son James had remained poor as a churchmouse; records of the Congress would presently show that even though the Monroes self-admittedly were dime-counters and dollar-squeezers, the unavoidable White House expenses had already put them in debt for about $20,000, in those times a formidable sum.

By then, certainly without monetary ambitions, James Monroe had been serving his country for forty-seven years—beginning just after his eighteenth birthday when he enlisted in a Virginia militia company that was promptly taken into the Continental Army. From that time onward, he had spent his life changing little chances to big deeds.

"Lizzie" Monroe could have added that at six her husband had taken over as "helpful boy" on his family's farm in Westmoreland County; the Monroes later moved to Loudon County, Virginia. At thirteen he was "rewarded" with two years at a private academy kept by Parson Archibald Campbell. At sixteen he began his brief tenure as a student at the College of William and Mary at Williamsburg, Virginia.

He recalled that on a serene morning while he was

attending Latin class, the town crier hurried by shouting out the news of the Battle of Lexington and Concord in distant Massachusetts. It did not seem distant to "Scholar" Monroe. He remembered how almost ten years earlier he had looked on while his father had joined a group of country and village neighbors on an overland tramp to Leedtown, a then widely known tobacco port on the Rappahannock River. At Leedtown the concerned volunteers had drafted and signed the Leedtown Resolutions. These were the first formal protest by American colonials against Great Britain's much disliked Stamp Act, which the bold protesters condemned as "taxation without representation."

The day after James Monroe's eighteenth birthday (April 28, 1776) British troops stationed at Williamsburg seized and confiscated the powder magazine or storagehouse which was maintained by the town for the protection of its citizens—from civil strife or marauders. On that basis the public powder magazine was regarded as a legitimate and necessary public facility. In protest Monroe joined fellow students and about forty other youths of the countryside in forming a "drilling company"—commanded by a stately, determined, and vocal citizen, Patrick Henry, Esquire. As a first venture in ardent exhibitionism, the volunteer force chose to hold their daily late-afternoon drill sessions on the palace green in full view of the resident British governor.

The drills, or as Monroe called them, the "show-off exercises," did not last long. Once ignited, the fire of revolution spread very rapidly. Well before the end of his sophomore year, "Jimmy" Monroe enlisted as a private soldier in the Virginia line, or militia. That ended his college days. Before his nineteenth birthday, he was a brevet lieutenant in the Continental Army and northward bound for crucial combat duty in what General George Washington, its Commander-in-Chief, described as "the obtaining theatre of decision."

Correctly, General Washington had pointed out that the British strategy was to divide her rebelling colonies into two sectors; first to conquer New York and New England, then, as convenient, to crush resistance in the lower Atlantic and the Southern colonies. Enlistee, brevet and line lieutenant, major, and finally Lieutenant-Colonel, Monroe did a remarkably great deal to frustrate that strategy. Throughout five and a half years, from White Plains to Valley Forge and Yorktown, and despite four minor wounds and a severe one suffered at the beginning of the Battle of Trenton, his combat record grew to be one of the most impressive in all the revolutionary armies.

But James Monroe left the recording to others. On discharge day he changed from a dedicated warrior to a dedicated peace-builder. At twenty-three he began reading and clerking in the Fredericksburg law office of Virginia's already renowned governor and statesman-at-large, Thomas Jefferson. From that arduous beginning, made the more so by the great pain of his shoulder-and-chest wound, Monroe launched himself on an exceptional career of public office-holding. This began with his election as a town councilman for Fredericksburg, then to a seat in the Virginia legislature where he presently was named a member of the Executive Council, then briefly to a seat in the Continental Congress. He returned to his native state to serve four terms as governor and to win election as a United States senator. He was sent as ranking United States envoy or minister to London, Paris, and Madrid. He next served in President Madison's cabinet as secretary of state, and during most of the War of 1812 he doubled as secretary of state and secretary of war.

Throughout his decades in public office he said a great deal about attaining peace and very little about war.

The one remembered exception occurred during his 1817 tour of New England and upstate New York as the newly inagurated fifth president of the United States. From Boston, where they arrived by sailing sloop, Monroe and his official party set out by overland stagecoach for a first look at inland New England, which had strongly supported his candidacy.

At Hanover, New Hampshire, where he was a most special guest of Dartmouth College, Monroe recognized the college president's wife as the volunteer nurse who had cared for him during and after the Battle of Trenton. The newly elected President wept unashamedly while recounting, perhaps for the first time in public, the highlights of his "five years plus of fighting and five months plus of almost dying" in the revolutionary war. Then, impulsively and publicly, he kissed the hostess, Mrs. Mary Wheelock, ". . . who nursed me through and saved my life at Trenton."

The shy and otherwise uncommon common-man president then stated firmly that he was and would ever remain a "peace-keeping servant" and that he promised to pray and labor to the end of making his presidency memorable as the "Era of Good Feelings." By December 2, 1823, most of the nation and much of the world could agree that James Monroe was keeping his promise.

2. The Monroe "Message"

ON THAT GRIM December morning in 1823 the aging President of the United States had completed his homework. With a great deal of help from the sharply-spoken John Quincy Adams, his secretary of state, and from other State Department "agents" and colleagues, Monroe had spent more than a month drafting what he believed to be his most meaningful and quite possibly his final message to the Congress.

It was a long communication, long enough to fill this book and part of another, and its scrawled text comprised a summary of its author's opinions and experiences from a half-century of public service. Monroe was not seeking to urge or sell specific laws or resolutions. Rather he sought to record a philosophy, a thoughtful statement of government principles and moral estimates that might endure much longer than he, or for that matter his present listeners, could expect to.

On this grim Tuesday morning the plainly dressed, plain-spoken president was calling at the Capitol to make himself available for questions or comments from congressmen who might be "up and around" as early as Monroe usually was. He had already delivered the manuscript to the Speaker of the House, who had assigned a clerk to read the script to the joint session of the Senate and the House of Representatives arranged for that afternoon.

The president was merely paying a courtesy call on his colleagues of the Congress; he would answer questions or arguments in person, for any who wished to question or argue. He would have preferred to read the message himself, but as he knew better than anyone else, his talents as a public speaker were meager and recently he had been afflicted with a throat infection that discouraged attempts at long speeches. He would therefore keep with the "official reader precedence."

As usual, his neighborly call was cordially received. Practically everybody liked James Monroe; he had almost unbelievably few enemies—"even fewer enemies," he reflected, "than dollars."

His arrival at the Capitol had the qualities of a homecomer's greeting in a country store. Congressmen clustered about him to shake hands and make small talk. When stately Virginia Senator John Randolph noted the depth of the snowed-on mud as measured by the president's boots, Monroe shed his great cloak and displayed a comparatively new suit, explaining that his daughter Lizzie and Rembrandt Peale, the presidential portrait painter, had "conspired and nagged" him into buying it.

A mood of acceptance already obtained with regard to the special message of which most members of the Congress as well as other principal government workers had already heard, at least indirectly. All were aware, or confident, that it would cover many of the momentous problems that confronted the still very young and very poor United States of America and its frequently stumbling toddler of a national government.

Most agreed that the hard-working, plain president had led remarkably well during hard and dangerous times. To cite only one reason for this common agreement: Monroe and his sharp-witted secretary of state, John Quincy Adams, had managed to keep the young country out of the deadly maelstrom of European power politics that followed the blood-smearing boundaries-wrecking Napoleonic wars. It was axiomatic that such "mighty grouches" as J. Q. Adams loved nobody but themselves and old, steady Jim Monroe.

Admittedly many congressmen favored their president because he was the almost unanimous choice of the American people. "Voting against Mr. Monroe is like voting against God," John Clymans, a young congressman from New York, had said in a floor speech; "it's possible but not politically feasible."

The slow-speaking, heavy-gaited president didn't particularly like that statement. After all, he was a humble man; he dressed, spoke, and otherwise lived the part. Members of Congress knew that he was as accessible as the fresh air. His White House fireplace, which he usually kindled and "logged" himself, was ringed with comfortable chairs; anyone who would speak with the president had only to call and sit and, again quoting Monroe, "spit out whatever he had to say."

It was no less common knowledge that the president asked modestly of Congress, supervised the expenditures of public money with remarkable care and competence, and usually got what he asked for.

His first term he had devoted to domestic problems

—such as building (or not building) public roads, river ports, and the first canals; also admitting new states, establishing new territories, extending the public mails, paying still unpaid war veterans, opening public lands for homesteading, and so on year after year. Again and again he had successfully supported then unpopular causes, such as establishing Indian treaties and founding, supplying, and protecting a first West African settlement for free Negroes.*

The fifth president had overlooked his upbringing and residence in the first of the slavery states and had signed into law the renowned Missouri Compromise which provided that thereafter all new states above 36 degrees 30 minutes north latitude would be admitted to the Union as nonslave, or "free" states. As an able lawyer and intensive student of the Constitution of the United States, Monroe doubted that the prevailing temper of the courts, particularly the Supreme Court, would accredit the then radical law as constitutional. In time the epochal Dred Scott decision would sustain that expert opinion. Even so, Monroe had signed the landmark bill into law, believing, as he stated, that American justice would eventually fall apace with "genuine American needs." Similarly the fifth president had fought quietly but effectively to stamp out the slave trade, from which many of his most powerful supporters took their livelihoods or wealth.

The Monroe popularity continued to survive heated controversies, and nobody could honestly doubt his amazing administrative competence. He and his cabinet and

---

* Some of the African settlers were being liberated from slavery in order to participate in the effort to establish a new nation for Negroes. The settlers were joining in renaming their seaport and capital, originally "Christopolis," to "Monrovia."

his other assistants were keeping a preponderantly poor, rural, sparsely settled, hot-tempered young nation out of war and free of debt. In accomplishing this, the president was working along, as the saying went, like an old-fashioned, people-loving, competent, ever-busy country storekeeper.

Time would prove that the simile was literal as well as figurative. Following his retirement from the nation's highest office, Monroe returned to his favorite Virginia county (Loudon) and to one of the lowliest of elective offices, that of justice of the peace. Then, following the death of his beloved wife, "Old Mr. America" on his seventieth birthday set forth for New York City, where he spent his final year helping his daughter and son-in-law establish and "keep" their store (a small department store).

The text of the lengthy message that would shortly be read to the two houses of Congress and other dignitaries of the national capital could be described as a treatise on another kind of storekeeping—international and interhemispheric in scope. Its highlights included nine principal points that the nation and the world would presently know as the Monroe Doctrine.

The Monroe Doctrine

1. The American continents, being free and independent, *are no longer open to colonization by European powers.*
2. We have never taken any part in European wars and politics, nor does it comport [agree] with our policy to do so.

3. *We shall consider any attempt by the European powers to extend their political systems to any part of this* [the American] *Hemisphere as dangerous to our peace and safety.*

4. We have not interfered and shall not interfere with the existing colonies of European powers.

5. *We shall consider any attempt by European powers to oppress or control in any other manner the free states of the Americas as an act unfriendly to the United States.*

6. Our policy has been and remains, *not to interfere with the internal concerns of Europe,* to recognize the *de facto* [actually existing] governments as legitimate, and to preserve friendly relations, when possible with honor, with all.

7. *Any attempt, in any form, to extend the European political system, which is not acceptable to the States South of us, to any part of this hemisphere, will endanger our peace and happiness.*

8. *The true policy of the United States is to leave the new States, which Spain can never subdue, to themselves.*

9. We hope that other powers will leave them [the newly born free nations of Latin America] to themselves.

Before the first three manuscript pages had been read all who knew Monroe were aware that this most unusual message was a personal document written with impersonal fervor and deep and perceptive awareness of the problems and perils then confronting the United States.

The opening pages recognizably paraphrased the first president's views regarding foreign policy and international relations. Monroe had included an almost verbatim restatement of the pivotal paragraph of George Washington's Farewell Address:

The great rule of conduct for us in regard to foreign nations is, in extending our commercial relations, to have with them as little *political* connection as possible. So far as we have already formed engagements let them be fulfilled with perfect good faith. Here let us stop.

Having indicated his esteem and reverence for his "first White House master," but without denying his strong and earlier disagreements with the first president, the message writer paid indirect tribute to the third president, Thomas Jefferson, but discreetly avoided the often-quoted statement (from Jefferson's first inaugural address) that "we are kindly separated by Nature and a wide ocean from the exterminating havoc of one quarter of the globe."

Deftly and clearly Monroe indicated his own studied conviction that, regardless of nature and the Atlantic Ocean, the prevailing havoc and lusts of colony-grabbing Europe did indeed imperil the Americas; the "wide ocean" was no longer wide enough to guarantee a safeguarding separation of the hemispheres.

Until James Monroe was fifty-three and had been twenty-eight years in government service, the United States had been the only consequential independent nation in the Western Hemisphere.

Abruptly this had changed. As of December 2, 1823, eight former colonies or parts of colonies in Latin America had declared themselves independent and sovereign nations. Coexistence with these borning American nations and protecting both them and the United States from rapacious seizure by European powers were now an absolute need and a prime condition for Pan-American survival and integrity.

Repeatedly Monroe noted that the God-created world of man is ever changing. But a unique and exceptionally imperiling epoch of change was in progress. During the previous months and as a thoughtful, longtime student of international affairs, Monroe had been making what he termed a studious survey of the rapidly changing Americas. In this painstaking task he had the help of his very able cabinet, particularly of the strongly opinionated John Quincy Adams, his secretary of state, whom many historians regard as the most brilliant and able American ever to hold that number one cabinet post. President Monroe also "reviewed" with the help of his great predecessor and friend, Thomas Jefferson, and of his small but able staff of "foreign agents." (This was an era of ministers, consuls, envoys, and emissaries or special agents rather than formal ambassadors.)

3. The Official
Onlooker

Monroe had made deft use of his earlier official experiences in observing foreign policy and the changing status of nations.

Back in 1811, while Monroe was Madison's secretary of state, a "congress of patriots" in the then colony of Venezuela had voted a declaration of independence from Spain and had chosen the adventurous Gertulio Miranda as their "liberation leader." But royalists had overcome the brave effort, and Miranda was left to die in a Spanish prison. At almost the same time the would-be Hidalgo revolution in Mexico was cruelly crushed by Spanish authorities. Murmurs of uprising were also being heard from more distant Buenos Aires and the mountainous Chilean lands to the west.

Immediately Monroe had managed to employ and dispatch "diplomatic agents" to Venezuela, Mexico, Buenos Aires, and Chile. This was the beginning of our diplomatic relations with Latin America. The then secretary of state Monroe thoughtfully explained his deep sympathy with the seekers of liberation from Spain. He pointed out (1) that Spain was severely restricting South

American trade with the outside world and among or between individual colonies, (2) that Spain was denying citizen rights of both the "territorials" (in greater part the native Indian peoples) and the Creoles (South American–born Spaniards), and (3) that like all other enlightened peoples, the Spanish Americans were feeling the urge to be and live as free men.

Then, during 1813, while the United States was harassed by the painful and unpopular War of 1812, the Venezuela-born Simón Bolívar took up the cause for which his friend Miranda had died. The slightly built liberator began persuading and leading his fellow Creoles to join in renewed quest of "liberty."

Bolívar's valiant efforts were benefitted by Napoleon's ruthless conquest of Spain, which was leaving Spanish America governed (or driven) only by the so-called viceroys, the representatives of the temporarily fallen Spanish crown.

During 1812 anti-Royalists in Spain set up at Cortes what they termed a Patriots' Government and invited all Spanish colonies to join the "Empire of Liberation." The effort did not succeed. British armies took the lead in driving Napoleon's forces out of Spain and opening the way for the return of Spain's Ferdinand VII. The reactionary emperor promptly dispatched a battle fleet to again break the "rebelliousness" of his South American colonies. But Simón Bolívar renewed his leadership of a peoples' revolt in what would become the republics of Venezuela, Colombia, and Ecuador.

In July 1816, while Monroe was beginning his victorious first campaign for the presidency, Buenos Aires, which included most of what is now Argentina, declared itself an independent nation. Its liberator was another native Spanish-American, General José San Martín, who had recruited a citizen army in the interior and shaped it into an effective combat force. While Bolívar continued to repulse the Spanish forces to the north, and as a renewed revolution smoldered in Mexico, General San Martín led his guerrilla army across the Andes, and soundly defeated Spain's Pacific outpost force, thereby opening the way for the liberation of Chile and Peru.

By 1823, the date of Monroe's historic annual message, eight newly formed Latin American countries had declared their independence from Spain: Buenos Aires (then usually spelled Buenoes Ayers); New Granada or Colombia (which then included what are now Venezuela and Ecuador); Chile; Peru, including what is now Bolivia; Santo Domingo (now the Dominican Republic and Haiti); the Confederation of Central America; the new "empire" of Mexico; and the "kingdom" of Brazil. Uruguay, earlier a territory of Brazil, was also in the borning. Monroe and Adams had already gained official United States recognition for four of the newcomers (Buenos Aires, New Granada, Chile, and Mexico) and were moving to obtain recognition for the others. They were confident that formal recognition of the new states as bona fide countries would provide them a degree of protection as well as status.

Spain still regarded the "new Americas" as rebellious colonies, and Great Britain, like the other European powers, had not officially recognized any of them.

Monroe and Adams also knew that the common people of the United States, and for that matter most of the members of Congress, still knew extremely little about the new states to the South. Some had heard of the fabled gold, silver, and other mineral wealth in Mexico and Peru.

Many more were acquainted with such Latin American products as cane sugar, coffee, and spices, which were being imported, principally from the West Indies. Otherwise, most Americans still knew practically nothing of Latin America.

Though most members of the Congress shared this extreme lack of knowledge, some were pointing out that the new states were quite unlike our own country. At least two had so-called emperors, and most of the others had single-party governments led by "strong men." (The term "dictator" was not yet in common use.) Other congressmen were airing their "understandings" that the new Latin American countries were most markedly influenced, politically as well as culturally, by European sources, even though Spain had largely withdrawn her military forces from South America.

Monroe could not entirely deny that "understanding," although he knew that it was not wholly true. His earlier experiences as presidential envoy to several European capitals, and his more recent studies, supported by John Quincy Adams's, confirmed the following beliefs:

France, once more a kingdom and the strongest of the Latin powers, was undeniably looking to Latin America with designs for again acquiring an American empire.

Great Britain, by then the world's leading maritime nation, was reaching out for advantageous colonies and naval stations all around the world. She had already taken over earlier Spanish holdings in the Caribbean— with beautiful and fertile Jamaica island as a trading base. By 1823 Britain was again on good terms with Spain and admittedly eager to build up trade with what had been Spanish America, and the British Empire was expanding powerfully.

There was another Old World development which Monroe's administration had found more immediately disturbing. This was the so-called Holy Alliance of Russia, Prussia, and Austria. Its professed goal was to withstand the ravages of the Napoleonic wars that had so profoundly upset the power balances of Europe. But the more basic and continuing purpose of the Holy Alliance, which Monroe in private termed the Unholy Alliance, was to uphold the so-called divine right of kings and to retard the growing movement toward peoples' governments. Its most heeded spokesman was Austria's Foreign Minister Prince Metternich, who eloquently preached that the survival of Europe depended upon the "legitimacy" of the already established governments and obedience to their royalties. Metternich insisted that the "virtuous nations" were duty bound to lead in preventing "populist revolts," wherever they might occur.

By the Treaty of November 20 (1815) Great Britain favored the Alliance at least to the extent of helping restore France's dwindling position in continental Europe. Three years later France, which was moving back into empire status, began to win the approval of the Holy Alliance by her willingness to stand against "revolutionary movements." By 1821 the Holy Alliance was trumpeting that it would permit no further "drastic changes" in any European governments.

However, at the so-called Congress of Verona the following year, when Russia, Prussia, and Austria proposed a formal treaty that required all principals to crush progressive movements within their own countries, Britain deftly withdrew. She could not stomach the preachment that representative government is incompatible with what Metternich had termed the "divine right of kings," or that the free press, the "most powerful means used by the supporters of the so-called rights of nations to the detriment of those of the Princes," must be repressed; further that the Christian religion should be used to keep the peoples in the passive obedience "which they owe to their Princes."

The Alliance was doing more than just spieling words. In Prussia protesting students were being severely punished. In what is now Italy, the valiant efforts of Naples to free itself from a tyrannical city-state king were abruptly crushed by Alliance members; France was being "authorized" to invade Spain and restore the latter's reactionary king-emperor.

Monroe and his advisors knew, of course, that the increasing throngs of Europeans who were seeking reforms in their own countries were looking ever more eagerly to the New World; also that the "Unholy Alliance" was looking West ever more threateningly. Czarist Russia, for example, was practically shouting her desire to extend her territorial claims from Alaska southward into the Oregon Territory and perhaps California.

On the more comforting side, Monroe was aware that Britain had a particularly astute foreign secretary, George Canning, who appreciated the possibilities and future importance of the United States as the "upcoming English-speaking power" and most useful British ally in the Western Hemisphere. Canning knew that the British Isles, particularly England, were already changing to a government of and for the people. Canning also looked on czarist Russia as the strongest enemy of the Pan-American progress toward independent governments. This point of view was supported by Czar Alexander's *ukase*, or decree (in 1821), that Russia's "American empire" should rightfully include not only the Alaska colony but most of the western coast of North America and control of the north Pacific and the Bering Sea. It also ordered American shipping not to come closer than a hundred miles to Russia's American-Pacific claims.

Although he privately discounted the bold, loud talk, Monroe had fully approved Secretary of State Adams's move to inform the czar's foreign minister, Baron von Tuyll, that the United States "would contest the right of Russia to *any* additional territorial establishment on this continent," and his repeating that "the American continents are no longer subjects for *any* new European colonial establishments." On July 22, 1823, Adams had repeated the stand even more firmly, and Britain's foreign secretary Canning officially indicated British agreement.

Several months before Monroe wrote his annual message of 1823, his cabinet, particularly Secretary of State Adams and Secretary of War John Calhoun, and other respected advisors, including former presidents Jefferson and Madison, had joined in serious discussions of the many threats of European infringement on the Americas. Monroe restated his "impression" that "we view any interference on the part of the European powers, and especially any attack on the Colonies [that is, on Latin America] as an attack on ourselves, presuming that if they succeeded . . . they would extend it to us. . . ."

From his letters to his two living presidential predecessors (Jefferson and Madison), one learns that Monroe had made a final decision as to the text of his forthcoming message. He was resolved upon a bold and open declaration of intentions by the United States rather than a joint message with Great Britain, as Foreign Secretary Canning had recommended. He was determined to speak as president of the United States and as an international champion of democracy, not as either a colleague or a critic of any European power.

Twenty-three days before the message of December 2, 1823, a spirited cabinet meeting had shown a majority in favor of joint declaration by the United States and Great Britain. Secretary Adams objected on the grounds that this would place Britain in a position to protest the acquisition of Spanish-claimed territory such as East Florida, which the United States had already obtained by treaty, and the Mexican province of Texas, which had already indicated a wish to join the United States. Adams also reiterated that Great Britain had not yet officially recognized any Latin American countries, whereas the United States had. William Wirt, the attorney general, asked whether the United States was willing to "fight"— literally to risk her life to support her president's convictions. Secretary of War Calhoun insisted that the Holy Alliance had ". . . an ultimate eye on us; they would, if not resisted, subdue South America . . . and we would have to fight on our own shores for our own institutions." Adams responded that our only safe course was to "disclaim" all interference by or from "Eurasia, . . . to make an American course and adhere inflexibly to that."

Many not actually present were in effective agreement; to name only two, New Hampshire's and Massachusetts' great orator-legislator Daniel Webster and Kentucky's Henry Clay. At the moment Clay was not even a member of the Congress, but the next January would find him returned to office and elected Speaker of the House.

Monroe had listened closely, accepted suggestions, including those contained in various letters and the fervent but thoughtful recommendations of John Quincy Adams.

But with great pains and care he had drafted his own message, keeping it, so he believed, "mild, respectful & friendly. . . ." And reasoning:

> If we look to the comparative strength and resources of Spain and those new Governments, and their distance from each other, it must be obvious that she can never subdue them. It is still the true policy of the United States to leave the parties to themselves, in the hope that other powers will pursue the same course. . . ."

Two days after the message was read, Monroe found time to write a letter to his renowned "advocate," Thomas Jefferson:

> . . . It has been done in mild, respectful & friendly manner. Had I omitted to put the country on guard, & anything had occurred of a serious character, I should probably have been censured, as it is they may look before them and what may be expedient. . . .

Certainly the "mild, respectful & friendly manner" was in keeping with the fact that the United States was still a comparatively small and poor nation. At the time her census was somewhere near 11.5 million. The War Department, which made the census, was invariably late with its homework. (Compiling the returns, many of them pencilled or crayoned on wrapping paper and all tallied by hand and simple arithmetic, required years and involved numerous errors and educated guesses.) About 85 percent of our people then lived on farms or in rural villages, most were poor, and few had seen the world beyond their home townships or, at most, counties. There were no large cities, or railroads, and few easily traveled roads. The Army was limited to tiny, ill-equipped patrol forces, and the Navy, although growing, was, as Monroe admitted, "valiant of heart but pennywhistle of tonnage." The progress of popular government was impressive. But the world's military power was still concentrated in Europe; the same held for industrial progress. American resources were principally its farm harvests and other raw materials.

As a distinguished war veteran and student of the military, Monroe was keenly aware of the limitations of his country's defensive and police powers. He was no less aware that the Atlantic Ocean was no longer a blockade between what he termed "the two spheres." Ships and merchandise were crossing the Atlantic in ever growing argosies; so were art, literature, and political ideologies. In greater part the traffic was two-way.

Other background facts were as self-evident as a country washday. The former Spanish colonies would never be taken back by Spain alone. A stronger power or powers would have to do the reconquering, if it were done. The United States would regard any such action as an unfriendly or hostile act. We would stand against "interference" by foreign powers. But we could not promise to keep our new American neighbor states from dividing themselves into smaller "pieces" or absorbing each other —indeed both processes were already in progress.

Other nations, including several that were more powerful militarily than the United States, already had extensive colonies in the American hemisphere. The Monroe Doctrine did not seek to take over or challenge any colonies already established.

Secretary Adams appeared to believe that most or all of the prevailing European colonies would somehow fade away. Monroe did not share that view. Even so, he did not favor trying to prohibit the transfer of already established colonies from one power to another. His aim was to prevent the creation of any new ones.

Monroe also insisted that the self-declared independent American nations be treated as such, granting that not all as yet were republics. He privately believed that in time all the Latin American countries would choose to be republics and so, as he said, "keep alive the flame of liberty." But that was their prerogative.

Monroe also sought to encourage trade with the newer Americas, to keep duties and regulations as liberal as possible. He recalled correctly that the desire to trade with the West Indies and Latin America were among the motives for waging the American Revolution. He believed ever so sincerely that the ways to market are ways to peace.

He was deeply conscious of the need for peace; he felt for peace as only a longtime battle veteran (and a severely wounded one) can. During the forty-eight years between the beginning of the American Revolution and December 1823, the Western Hemisphere as a whole had known only two years of peace—1783 and 1791. Monroe was unhappily aware that the new Latin American countries were already quarreling among themselves, but he regarded this as "human behavior," or "family spats," not as "truly serious." He favored letting people solve their own differences where possible. He insisted that what would live on as the Monroe Doctrine was not international law and not a device for hemisphere domination by the United States.

James Monroe believed all the foregoing. But what would others think? As he had hoped and expected, his message was generally well received in the United States.

It was cordially accepted by London but it was opposed or ridiculed by most European capitals.

British Foreign Minister Canning said in effect, "precisely what I was saying." His one regret was that it could not have been a joint declaration of the United States and his own country. The London press mostly agreed that the message "dispersed joy, exultation, and gratitude over all free men of Europe." Royal Spain was openly angered. France's minister for foreign affairs, Chateaubriand, cried out that "Monroe's Madness" ought to be resisted by all powers with either territorial or commercial interests in the Americas.

L'Etoile, then the leading Parisian newspaper, scoffed, "Mr. Monroe is the temporary president of a republic situated on the eastern coast of North America. . . . On what title then are the two Americas from Hudson's Bay to Cape Horn now under its immediate control?"

From Vienna the tottering Prince Metternich condemned the Doctrine bitterly.

Official London responded by making a beginning at recognizing the new Latin American republics. When the Spanish government retorted that its former colonies were "as infants in strength but old in crime supported by ambition and defended by blood and anarchy," Canning scoffed. Monroe, we are told, indulged in a "broad, gentle smile." (Eliza Monroe observed that when her husband smiled, it had to be a broad smile; his mouth wasn't made for smallness.)

From Latin America, Simón Bolívar expressed his appreciation. Brazil forwarded thanks and stated her willingness to join the United States in an "offensive-defensive" alliance. Many newspapers in the United States agreed that the Monroe message had helped arouse aware-

PRESIDENT'S MESSAGE.

Yesterday, at two o'clock, the PRESIDENT OF THE UNITED STATES transmitted to both Houses of Congress, by the hands of his Private Secretary, the following

MESSAGE:

*Fellow-Citizens of the Senate
and House of Representatives:*

Many important subjects will claim your attention during the present session, of which I shall endeavor to give, in aid of your deliberations, a just idea in this communication. I undertake this duty with diffidence, from the vast extent of the interests on which I have to treat, and of their great importance to every portion of our Union. I enter on it with zeal, from a thorough conviction that there never was a period, since the establishment of our Revolution, when, regarding the condition of the civilized world, and its bearing on us, there was greater necessity for devotion in the public servants to their respective duties, or for virtue, patriotism, and union, in our constituents.

Meeting in you a new Congress, I deem it proper to present this view of public affairs in greater detail than might otherwise be necessary. I do it, however, with peculiar satisfaction, from a knowledge that, in this respect, I shall comply more fully with the sound principles of our government. The people being with us exclusively the sovereign, it is indispensable that full information be laid before them on all important subjects, to enable them to exercise that high power with complete effect. If kept in the dark, they must be incompetent to it. We are all liable to error, and those who are engaged in the management of public affairs, are more subject to excitement, and to be led astray by their particular interests and passions, than the great body of our constituents, who, being at home, in the pursuit of their ordinary avocations, are calm but deeply

his Imperial Majesty to the government of Great Britain, which has likewise been acceded to. The government of the United States has been desirous, by this friendly proceeding, of manifesting the great value which they have invariably attached to the friendship of the Emperor, and their solicitude to cultivate the best understanding with his government. In the discussions to which this interest has given rise, and in the arrangements by which they may terminate, the occasion has been judged proper, for asserting, as a principle in which the rights and interests of the United States are involved, that the American continents, by the free and independent condition which they have assumed and maintain, are henceforth not to be considered as subjects for future colonization by any European powers.

Since the close of the last session of Congress, the Commissioners and Arbitrators for ascertaining and determining the amount of indemnification which may be due to citizens of the United States, under the decision of his Imperial Majesty the Emperor of Russia, in conformity to the convention concluded at St. Petersburg, on the 12th of July, one thousand eight hundred and twenty-two, have assembled in this city, and organized themselves as a board, for the performance of the duties assigned to them by that treaty. The commission constituted under the eleventh article of the treaty of the twenty-second of February, eighteen hundred and nineteen, between the United States and Spain, is also in session here; and, as the term of three years, limited by the treaty, for the execution of the trust, will expire before the period of the next regular meeting of Congress, the attention of the Legislature will be drawn to the measures which may be necessary to accomplish the objects for which the commission was instituted.

In compliance with a resolution of the House of Representatives, adopted at their last session, instructions have been given to all the Ministers of the United States, accredited to the powers of Europe and America, to propose the proscription of the African slave trade, by classing it under the denomination, and inflicting on its perpetrators the punishment, of piracy. Should this proposal be acceded to, it is not doubted, that this odious and criminal practice will be promptly and entirely suppressed. It is earnestly hoped that it will be acceded to, from the firm belief that it is the most effectual expedient that can be adopted for the purpose.

Reproduction of the Monroe Message from the Washington *National Intelligencer* for December 3, 1823. Reproduced from the collections of the Library of Congress.

ness of the growing international consequence of the young nation and had bolstered public self-confidence in the role of the United States, not only as a big brother (or sister) of the other Americas, but as a strong force in international life.

The first important aftermath of the doctrine was the czar's withdrawal of Russia's claims on the American Pacific Coast north of north latitude 51 degrees, including "rights" on a hundred miles of offshore waters and the foolish claim to the north Pacific and the Bering Sea as exclusive Russian domain. By the peaceful Treaty of 1824, Imperial Russia forfeited the unreasonable claims and accepted north latitude 54 degrees 40 minutes as the southern limit of Russia-in-North-America. This, of course, affirmed Russia's possession of Alaska, but freed the Oregon Territory and California from Russian claims. The treaty also sustained the Monroe Doctrine's stand against the founding of new colonies in the American hemisphere.

Political support kept growing at home. Early in 1824, Henry Clay, as Speaker of the House of Representatives, moved to introduce a joint resolution "strengthening the wording of the Monroe Doctrine," and making the "federal legislative department a rightful sharer in its perpetuation." Monroe, meanwhile, was successfully completing his final year as president. John Quincy Adams, who was winning election as sixth president, had already chosen Henry Clay as his secretary of state. An extremely able replacement team was taking the field.

4. "Forgive Us Our Trespasses"

In 1831 in New York City, James Monroe died of what his doctors termed "an affliction of breathing," and described as an aftermath of his Battle of Trenton wound.

Since retiring from the presidency in March 1825, "Old Mr. America" had carried on many useful works, including serving as a justice of the peace, as a trustee of the University of Virginia and as president of the American Colonization Society. This society continued to sponsor the settlement of freed Negroes in West Africa's Liberia, by then a commonwealth and presently to become the first African republic. He had helped his "young folks" set up their store on Houston Street in Manhattan, and he had kept up what he termed a warm advising friendship with his presidential successor, John Quincy Adams.

Monroe continued to believe that his 1823 message was his most lasting accomplishment. He was grateful for the works and words of its many supporters, led by John Quincy Adams, Henry Clay, and John Calhoun, all "enduring statesmen," and many congressmen, including the eloquent Daniel Webster.

But from time to time Monroe's personal letters had

41

expressed concern regarding the foreseeable future of the Doctrine. Its painstaking writer did not expect that the Congress would, as he said, "keep everlastingly warm on the subject." His persisting hope was that the "frame of mind" would live on, stay adaptable to changing times and parties (the conservative Whigs were then in power), and serve to discourage or "scare away" European infringement on the Americas. He repeated that the Doctrine is essentially a working tool, and asked that it be used as such and not be merely "exclaimed about."

During 1826, the second year of Monroe's busy retirement, President Adams again strongly supported the Doctrine in his official greeting to the Panama Congress, the first assembly or convention of American states. The sixth president assured the assembly of his determination to keep the Doctrine "vividly alive and not shelved"; as needs required, he would move to put teeth into it.

Monroe had not anticipated any really drastic showdown or need for "teeth" during his own lifetime. His country by then was leaping into adolescence, with plenty of "jumping room" already available. The million square miles of the Louisiana Territory were beginning to take form as new states and territories. United States foreign trade and shipping were multiplying, also, but the prevailing directions were toward Europe and the Far East and other Pacific lands rather than Latin America.

The newer American nations were not "growing up" as rapidly as Monroe had hoped and predicted; he noted that instead of joining together, several were breaking apart. One instance was Colombia. That very beautiful country, which had worked so hard to obtain the first official recognition, was dividing herself into three—New Granada (substantially the present Colombia), Venezuela, and Ecuador. Peru had divided herself by sprouting Bolivia. But at least Spain was ceasing to protest loudly; Monroe predicted that within another five years Imperial Spain would officially recognize all her former South American colonies as sovereign nations.

Once more, "Old Mr. America" predicted correctly. He also foresaw that the big Mexican province of Texas, where a number of United States citizens were settling, would shortly be breaking away from Mexico. Monroe noted wisely that nations and families are like that; the Doctrine had not sought to keep new nations from leaving their earlier nests or homelands. Even so, he repeatedly warned of the possibility that the Doctrine's homeland and espouser, the United States, might be the most harmful violator. In his final letter to Thomas Jefferson, who died before the stagecoach-mail letter from New York reached him, Monroe mentioned the disquieting thought, and inserted from the Lord's Prayer: "Forgive us our trespasses as we forgive those who trespass against us."

While Monroe was in his final illness, the first conspicuous violations of the Doctrine occurred, with Great Britain the offender. By then, Britain was unquestionably the strongest, most influential European power. In a baffling storm of arguments, charges, and countercharges, and without heeding the vehement protests of what is now Argentina, Britain occupied and presently took over the Falkland Islands, a fisherman's haven in the ever-stormy south Atlantic east of Patagonia. Britain did not retract; the Monroe Doctrine's slate was visibly smudged.

However, this first smudge was being offset by a real if foot-dragging acceptance in the then distant Pacific. During his first presidential term Monroe had spoken appreciatively of the "peaceable Sandwich Islands [later renamed the Hawaiian Islands] in the Great Western Ocean, known to whalers and traders but not to Washington City." (The occasion for this reflection, in 1819, was a first party of Boston missionaries who had set out for these beautiful islands.)

During 1826 President Adams sent an official agent to the islands to "serve for American commerce and seamen." He also pointed out that the "philosophy" of the Monroe Doctrine could and should be extended to any area of "Pan American significance," actual or forthcoming. By then both Britain and France had made what Adams termed "gun-point treaties" with various native chiefs of the islands, forcing them to acknowledge foreign "protectorates."

By 1842 a respected British trade leader, Sir George Simpson, then director-general, or "governor," of the powerful Hudson's Bay Company, appealed to his own country, to France, and to the United States for fair and gracious treatment and continued independence for. the "Sandwiches." The then U.S. secretary of state, Daniel Webster, concurred warmly and persuaded his president, John Tyler, to advise the Congress and the world at large that in keeping with the Monroe Doctrine, ". . . any attempt to take possession of the islands, colonize them, and subvert the native government [would] create dissatisfaction on the part of the United States." The United States Congress promptly enacted a resolution, which clearly held that the Doctrine is applicable to the Eastern Hemisphere as well as the Western.

Five years later Daniel Webster hotly rebuked France for the outrageous action of one of her Pacific naval forces, the de Tromelin Squadron, which had ruthlessly attacked the island's capital, shelling and burning several of its buildings. Louis Napoleon, then warming the presidential chair of France preparatory to changing it to an emperor's throne, responded with a "deed of cession" making the islands a protectorate of the United States. The shrewd Yankee secretary of state recognized the move as a trick to make the United States a violator of her own accepted doctrine; Webster rejected the move and repeated that so far as his country was concerned, the Sandwich Islands would remain "free and self-sovereign."

Ironically, almost a half-century later, a group of American sugar companies, which by then largely dominated the islands, made a loud clamor for their official annexation to the United States. President Grover Cleveland sidestepped the issue. But during July 1898, as the Spanish-American War, which was openly in violation of both the text and principles of the Monroe Doctrine, neared its end, the Sandwich, alias Hawaiian, Islands were formally annexed by the United States. The question of conflict with the Monroe Doctrine was: Had a majority, or even a substantial number of the Islands' peoples actually approved the move of the sugar companies? If the answer was an honest yes, then there was no violation. But the majority was not given a choice.

Returning to the middle decades of the nineteenth century, which Daniel Webster knew so well and James Monroe foresaw with notable correctness, another complex, far-reaching, and foot-dragging violation was in progress.

Here again the violator was Great Britain. The opening scene was the jungle-strewn Caribbean coastlands of Central America—originally named the Miskito Coast (for the black Indians who lived there). For reasons more feelable than literate, the name had been changed to the Mosquito Coast. British merchant ships had first used the seafront as a refuge from pirates or buccaneers. Later timber firms had obtained permission from Spain to take mahogany and other fine woods from the area.

During 1835 settlers in and around the shallow-water port of Belize set up a local government which they named British Honduras and for which they claimed the coastal front south of the San Juan River. The British Foreign Office "accredited" the claim and directed Her Majesty's Navy to take over and aid San Juan village and several offshore islands, declaring the entire area a British protectorate. The Central American states, by then separated and duly recognized as independent republics, protested strongly, pointing out in Monroe's words that a European power was oppressing them and "controlling their destinies." It was a lengthy controversy to which, for reasons shortly to be noted, the United States turned a blind eye.

During 1860 Britain gave up her claim to the entire Mosquito Coast, but insisted that British Honduras, regardless of the protest and prior claims of Guatemala, Honduras, and Nicaragua, remain a British colony.

This action was in open violation of the Monroe Doctrine, which clearly prohibits the establishment of New World colonies subsequent to December 2, 1823. But the move by Great Britain had a still greater consequence. With British Honduras as a fulcrum, Britain was in position to take part in building, operating, and supervising the proposed canal linking the Atlantic and Pacific, a facility which could profoundly affect the economic and political future of much or all of the Western Hemisphere.

During 1846 Great Britain moved boldly to set up a treaty with Colombia whereby Britain and, as she saw fit, another European power, would be permitted to effect or oversee the building of such a canal across the Isthmus of Panama, then a territory of Colombia. In the same treaty the government at Bogota also granted permission for building a railroad across the Panama Narrows on the same terms. Undeniably the treaty violated both the principles and the specific terms of the Monroe Doctrine; it was an action by a European power to control or unduly influence the sovereignty of a free state of the Americas.

The disturbing picture was worsened by still uglier violations by the United States. The story here was one of the blackest in American history. It dealt with the truly deplorable Mexican War, which opened early in 1846 with a cruel, bloody, and punitive invasion of that neighbor nation by presidential orders—without a declaration of war by the Congress, as specifically required by the Constitution of the United States.

For the first time, many graduates of the United States Military Academy at West Point and other respected military personnel resigned their commissions in an Army they saw being used so dishonorably.

In 1844 James K. Polk, a handsome, strong-willed North Carolina-born Tennesseean, had won election as the eleventh president of the United States. Polk's platform favored "expansionism"—that is, adding to the land possessions of the United States by any means at hand. He made the annexation of Texas and its admission to the Union as a slavery state a first plank of his platform.

Henry Clay, as the nominee of the Whig party, stood for orderly growth within the prevailing boundaries and honoring the Monroe Doctrine, which he cited as a hall-mark of his own public career. The slavery issue figured strongly: Polk favored slavery and increasing the number of states and territories that permitted it.

He was keenly aware that most of Latin America op-posed slavery; the first constitutions of most of the newer American states prohibited it. The United States was a quarter century behind her neighbors in this regard. Even the colonies were being ridded of the curse of slavery. During the 1830s Britain had effected the freeing of slaves in Jamaica; and even reactionary Spain was moving to do away with slavery in Cuba. In his time Monroe had opposed the slave trade and as president had fought it almost to a standstill. But the ambitious, hard-willed Polk succeeded in restoring sentiment in favor of slavery while also advocating the extension of "slave territory."

In this and other respects Polk had gauged his po-litical following shrewdly. On March 4, 1845, a few hours before he took his oath of office as president, the Con-gress enacted a joint resolution to annex Texas. Mexico's strong and understandable protests were of no avail. The expansionists held that Texas, which was already officially recognized by the United States as an independent re-public, could choose its own course, including entry into the Union—a proceeding not in violation of the Mon-roe Doctrine.

However, in his tough inaugural address, Polk, even while declaiming his devotion to the Monroe Doctrine, clearly indicated his desire to annex California and Cuba. At the time, Cuba was Spain's most important New World colony. This, of course, was in open violation of the prin-ciples of the Doctrine. The new president strongly, if somewhat less than truthfully, insisted: "The United

States is already almost surrounded by the possessions of European powers; the Canadas, New Brunswick and Nova Scotia, the islands in the American seas, with Texas trammelled by treaties [mostly with Mexico], would complete the circle."

The annexation of Texas inevitably kindled the dispute with Mexico. Seizing on still unsettled boundary claims between Texas and Mexico as provocation, Polk ordered two combat forces of the United States Army into upper Mexico and readied a third for guerrilla-style or "cross-country" invasion of the huge northern frontier which the United States would shortly take over as "New Mexico Territory."

It was our first major war to have been begun in open defiance of the provision of our Constitution which directs that war can be declared only by the Congress. This one was far advanced, many believe, before the Congress made a "legal declaration." Mexico's forces were thinly spread and poorly equipped; although they fought bravely they were clearly overpowered by the invading "Gringoes" even before the United States officially declared war. On the whole, the pretext of causes was flimsy. The fact that the boundaries between Texas and its mother country had not been "finalized" merely repeated that in those times many American boundaries, including several of the United States, were not adequately or finally defined. The charges of Mexican "lawlessness" along the still theoretic boundaries were largely yammerings; claims that (like the United States) Mexico was not able to maintain law and order on all her frontiers.

The close of the most regrettable Mexican War saw the United States blatantly defying the Monroe Doctrine by making a huge land grab, wholly without consent of the resident peoples. The takeover of the New Mexico Territory, a swath stretching from El Paso to the Pacific, was the more deplorable because by prevailing laws and plans it would almost double the available "slavery territory."

The Treaty of Guadalupe-Hildalgo (February 2, 1848) which formally closed the Mexican War, was in almost total defiance of both text and spirit of the Monroe Doctrine. Its ink was barely dry when Polk recommended the seizure and annexation of Mexico's Yucatan Peninsula—allegedly to "protect" its "good people" (the white immigrants), from its "bad people," who almost had to be the native Indians. Fortunately in this instance the "grin-and-grab" routine did not obtain. One reason was that the non-Indian minority in Yucatan was apparently willing to have the peninsula attached to the United States, Great Britain, or Spain on a taker-keeper basis. Whatever its other merits or demerits, the minority and never official recommendation was in flagrant contradiction of both the terms and spirit of the Monroe Doctrine. The immediate reaction in official Washington was to encourage both the Senate and the House of Representatives to review and reappraise the Doctrine as a bona fide guide to sound foreign policy.

Even while the Polk administration continued to defame and threaten Mexico, the proposal to annex Yucatan brought out some notable counterquestions. One was, could or would this most revered foreign policy document authorize any American body politic to accept the domination or outright annexation by a foreign power, whether European or American? The mood of the Congress seemed to indicate that the answer was yes, as regards the United States, but no if the takeover were to be effected by a European power. Others argued that the identity of the annexing country was not of decisive importance; the real test was whether or not the transfer of sovereignty might presently or eventually prove to be harmful to the best interests of the United States. Clearly what John Calhoun had termed the good neighbors "attitude" of James Monroe was not sufficiently in evidence. But fortunately the Yucatan controversy was not solid enough to endure. In essence it was a highly localized and distinctly childish spat that presently faded away.

But the same did not hold for the more complex question of the proposed canal between the two great oceans. In his preoccupation with rabble-rousing at the expense of Mexico, Polk suggested that the canal issue could be "negotiated." The "storm-maker" from Tennessee and North Carolina did not explain just how he proposed to negotiate, but one of his envoys proceeded to demonstrate. Elijah Hise, representing himself as a "special emissary of the President," boldly and without bothering to seek the approval of the United States Senate, maneuvered a "treaty" with Nicaragua. This provided that the United States government might build, or contract with an American company to build, an interoceanic canal across Nicaragua using the San Juan River of that country as its throughway.

Britain, of course, heard of the antic, protested loudly, charged underhanded violation of the Monroe Doctrine, and began to use her consuls and other diplomats in Central America to enlarge the protest. The outcome included the Clayton-Bulwer Treaty of 1850, another flagrant contradiction of the Monroe Doctrine. The treaty provided that the United States and Britain might together build and jointly control, with the assistance of another European power as required, an intero-

ceanic canal, guaranteeing its "neutrality" and the privilege of all legitimate shipping to make use of it. Certainly
Monroe's great message would deny permitting a non-
American power, perhaps two non-American powers, to
be parties in an enterprise which could profoundly affect
the destinies of most or all of the American nations.

There were other serious doubts regarding the wisdom and honesty of the Clayton-Bulwer Treaty, but there
was none at all about the needs for such a canal, including
the United States' very special needs. The violent seizure
of the huge Mexican territory, which so obviously contradicted the basic principles of the Doctrine, and the
annexation of Texas, California, and the Oregon Territory (which was not in direct violation of the Doctrine)
multiplied the needs for an interoceanic passage. The
California gold rush (beginning in 1848) produced a more
specific need and caused public clamor. Shippers and
naval spokesmen joined in a chorus of "Give us a canal."

Quietly, during 1850 and following Polk's single, noisy
term as president, the United States government began
building a railroad across the Panama Narrows, and five
years later completed the "marvelous midget." Although
successful, the pint-size trans-Isthmus railroad was not an
adequate solution. The United States still lacked a transcontinental railroad and had appallingly few intersec-
tional roads. Reaching "Cal-i-forn-i-yay" by ship meant a
long, storm-endangered voyage through the "roaring for-
ties" around the far tip of South America. The toils and
dangers of land crossings of lower Central America were
still not surely removed. Going West by wagon train
abounded in privation and danger. The Americas, and the
United States in particular, needed an interoceanic canal
very badly. But the fulfillment of the need required a new

reach, indeed, a new concept of common-good internationalism. Could the Monroe Doctrine direct this?

Many, including the aging John Calhoun, who had
served Monroe so ably as counselor and secretary of war,
and Daniel Webster, who had revered Monroe as his
most special hero, were confident that the answer was
yes.

But fate and other high officials who piously praised
the Doctrine while willfully violating it, were boldly eras-
ing the "yes." If Polk had used the Doctrine poorly, two
of his eventual successors would be abusing it even more
—if that were possible.

These two were the one-term, strong-willed, and
largely incompetent presidents, Pierce and Buchanan, who
steered collision courses from March 1853 until March
1861—when the terrible Civil War was already under
way.

Both Franklin Pierce of New Hampshire, the four-
teenth president, and James Buchanan of Pennsylvania,
the fifteenth, were lawyer politicians with long tenures in
Congress. Both were Democrats who sought followings
from those who favored slavery and those who opposed
it. Both sought to take political advantage of prevailing
national trends, however regrettable, and both paid lip
service to the Monroe Doctrine while openly defying its
principles. Pierce had been a politically commissioned
"general" in the Mexican War. Buchanan had been Pierce's
ambassador to Great Britain and before that Polk's secretary of state. As freshman congressmen the pair had
shared the common experience of being Polk-style "slap-
'em-downers."

Buchanan, as mentioned, had had opportunity to
learn of internationalism. He recalled that as a young

congressman he had been "inspired" by his personal friendship with "the great Monroe," but the inspiration apparently had not taken.

Pierce, on the contrary, had pushed ahead politically without heed of foreign policy or even pretending a knowledge of international affairs. He had gained the highest office by openly catering to the essentially selfish appetite for expanding United States boundaries for the special benefit of special groups. The politicians' phrase for this was "manifest destiny," or stated more honestly—"get while the getting's good."

In his inaugural address, while emphatically praising the Monroe Doctrine, Pierce literally shouted his intentions to defy it:

> The policy of my administration shall not be controlled by any timid forebodings of evil from expansion. . . . Our attitude as a nation and our position on the globe render the acquisition of certain possessions not within our jurisdiction eminently important for our protection, if not in the future essential for preservation of the rights of commerce and the peace of the world. . . .

One outcome was the so-called Ostend Manifesto of 1854. Its text was not written by the president. Rather it was the brainchild, to use the term loosely, of three Pierce-appointed diplomats, the United States minister to Great Britain, James Buchanan (who would be the next president), and Messrs. Soule and Mason, the ministers to Spain and France, respectively. They proposed that, as a measure of self-protection, the United States should next take over Cuba, first offering to buy the island from Spain, but failing that to seize it by force. The Manifesto added that the seizure of Cuba (and, perhaps, any other coveted land) would be:

> . . . on the very same principle that would justify an individual in tearing down the burning house of his neighbor if there were no other means of preventing the flames from destroying his own home. . . .

The ludicrous sentiment flatly contradicted the text and spirit of the Monroe Doctrine and failed conspicuously to note that, at least at the time, Cuba was not "burning." In fact, the imperial government of Spain and the colonial government of Cuba were striving to bring improvements to the beautiful "Pearl of the Antilles," including ridding it of slavery. Progress was sufficient to cause alarm to proslavery politicians and lobbyists in the United States who foresaw that ridding Cuba of slavery would further strengthen the abolitionist movement in the United States.

Powerful though they were, the proslavery interests were not able wholly to dominate the Congress. The Ostend Manifesto failed to win acceptance, but Pierce and his White House successor kept on trying to take over Cuba.

For the supporters of the Monroe Doctrine the bold, loud efforts were discomfiting. Many legislators were pointing out that for the United States to take over Cuba would necessarily demonstrate that the Monroe Doctrine could be killed by many small bullets as surely as by one big one.

The "small bullets" continued to pour forth from official Washington. The Pierce administration had succeeded in making what its vocal opposition called the shotgun purchase of a transcontinental railroad right-of-way across upper Mexico. (It was being pointed out that not a cent of the $10 million purchase price actually reached the Mexican capital.)

During the first year of the Pierce presidency another regrettable flouting of the spirit of the Doctrine occurred. The scene was Paraguay, one of the weakest and most remote of the South American nations. The small wilderness republic had sought to close the channel of her Parana River in order to protect her citizens from the maraudings of river outlaws. During 1858 a United States ship, the *Water Witch*, had defied the entirely lawful orders of the Paraguayan government and had set out up the river. Reportedly the *Water Witch* was fired on by a guarding military force. Without investigating the facts, "Washington" (by then Buchanan was president) dispatched a squadron of seventeen naval craft to "crush the defiant action" and to "prove to the world . . . that the United States will not be defied by any South American State." The victim state could only yield to the overwhelming military force.

The slaughter of the Monroe Doctrine with small bullets continued. Earlier in the 1850s a profitable trade in a superior natural fertilizer called guano had come into being. The accumulation of organically rich seabird manure usually occurs on rocky offshore islands. Peru's Lobos Islands, directly off the coast, were especially rich in this resource. Peru protested that United States citizens were removing huge quantities of the guano without payment or lawful permission. "Washington" replied that the Lobos were "barren lands" and that "first comers" had the right to occupy them and harvest their resources; also that the free takers should be duly protected by their government.

When Peru repeated her protests, Pierce refused to listen. Instead, he recommended and during 1856 gained Congressional enactment of what many still regard as the most outrageous of all our federal statutes. Fittingly, it was nicknamed the Bird Manure Law:

> Whenever any citizen of the United States discovers a deposit of guano on any island, rock or key . . . not occupied by the citizens of any other government and takes peaceable possession thereof, and occupies the same, such island, rock or key may, at the direction of the President, be considered as appertaining to the United States. . . .

Certainly the implications were hurting the spirit and effectiveness of the Monroe Doctrine. In simplest language they were: Even if a resource and its lands are properly and lawfully yours, if you are not at this instant occupying and using them, your rights of ownership are officially denied; any alien or passerby may take over as if he were the owner; he can take over as he chooses and abandon as he sees fit without payment or responsibility.

Fortunately, no Latin American state responded in kind. Even so, the Monroe Doctrine was being used badly. Another most regrettable instance was the appearance of the so-called Soldiers of Fortune, for the most part brazen scoundrels and scofflaws who invaded, defiled, and otherwise injured and embarrassed various Latin American countries, particularly those of Central America. The most notorious of these trespassers was a General William Walker. His military title was fake, but his ruthless sorties with bandit gangs were tragically real. By coincidence Walker began taking the limelight as Pierce took over the presidency. During 1855, with the open aid of Cornelius

Vanderbilt, a New York banker who then controlled a monopoly transit service across the "narrows" of Nicaragua, the self-commissioned "general" took total possession of that beautiful, exploited little country. Walker next took the lead in saddling Nicaragua with a fraudulent government, mostly of fellow felons. In defiance of the Monroe Doctrine, the Pierce administration recognized the Walker-Vanderbilt mob as a good-faith government.

That looked and smelled like the lowest attainable depth of degradation of the Monroe Doctrine, but it wasn't. Buchanan, the next president of the United States saw to that. While he piously stated his esteem and reverence for the Doctrine and for his "noble friend, James Monroe," James Buchanan set about fanning the fires of "manifest destiny."

While resuming his propaganda for seizing Cuba and presumably other Caribbean colonies, Buchanan also indulged in tirades of abuse and threats regarding Mexico. During 1858, his first full year in the presidency, the Pennsylvanian loudly charged that "lawless factions" in northern Mexico were "menacing" our citizens and urged that the United States "assume military occupation" of the northern areas of the Mexican states of Sonora and Chihuahua. Late in 1859 he asked Congress for authority "to employ a sufficient military force to enter Mexico for the purpose of obtaining indemnity for the past and security for the future. . . ." This implied a resumption of total conquest.

Fortunately the majority of the Congress did not approve what seemed to be a manufactured attempt to divert attention from an even worse calamity. By then the United States was on the verge of the Civil War. There was evidence that Buchanan was using his angry abuse of our southern neighbor to veil his own inability to deal with the anger and militancy that were beginning to tear apart our country.

During the following December (1860) when, South Carolina openly withdrew from the Union and so signaled the beginning of the Civil War, Buchanan renewed his abusive condemnations of Mexico and Colombia, even while watching his own country break apart and plunge into bloody chaos.

5. The Phoenix

As THE CIVIL WAR flamed, the Monroe Doctrine appeared to be wholly dead. Its abuses had tended to establish the fallacies (1) that every American nation ought to have a government exactly like that of the United States and (2) that although European powers must not seize American territory, the United States was somehow justified in seizing any territory in the hemisphere, and in making treaties, however imperiling or hurtful, with any European power, so long as self-helping public officials of the United States regarded them as advantageous. Fortunately, not all politicians agreed. The new Republican party, in its convention of 1856, had described the Ostend Manifesto and what followed it as "the highwayman's plea that *might* makes *right*," adding that from Polk's administration through Pierce's, Latin America had much less to fear from Europe than from the United States.

On March 4, 1861, when Abraham Lincoln became president, with the capable and outspoken William H. Seward as his secretary of state, the Monroe Doctrine began to show a glimmering of life and the promise of resurrection. Seward bluntly declared that the Democratic party's "policy of annexation" had been a wholly immoral scheme for enlarging the slaveholding areas of the United States.

Burdened by the devastating Civil War, Lincoln dropped plans for building the Panama Canal and sought to restore friendly relations with Mexico and Latin America as a whole. His efforts met distinctly friendly responses. By way of his secretary of state, President Lincoln accepted openly the Monroe thesis that every Latin American government "has the right to establish and maintain its own government without intervention, intrusion or influence from foreign nations, *and especially from the United States.*"

The Lincoln administration also moved successfully to gain United States recognition of the two Negro republics, Haiti and Liberia—the latter, the only African republic, had waited fourteen years for recognition by the United States.

But fate would not permit Abraham Lincoln to serve as a peacetime president. The Civil War was actually begun before he could take his oath of office, and the chilling, killing war shadows were reaching far beyond his nation. During his first year as president the long hovering nightmare of a European takeover of an American nation changed to distressing reality. Again Mexico was the victim; France, abetted by both Britain and Spain, boldly undertook "to control the destinies of an American power."

To make matters worse, the three offending powers added to the list of less serious violations. Spain withdrew her troops from Veracruz, Mexico and dispatched them to strike down a peoples' revolt in progress on the island of Santo Domingo. Next the wavery Spanish crown opened a loud and bitter quarrel with Peru, insolently seizing her former colony's Chincha Islands, and angrily declaring war against Chile. The strife was comparatively shortlived, and again Spain lost.

But the French aggression was especially ominous. The brilliant Indian leader and patriot Benito Juarez was then the legitimate president of Mexico. His numerous problems included settling his country's debts, including those contracted by his unstable predecessors and rivals. Britain had refused to recognize Juarez's administration, declaring that he had evaded debts and other "responsibilities" to British subjects. Spain was openly unfriendly toward Juarez's administration.

France, under Napoleon III, angrily condemned the Juarez leadership for not having honored the so-called Jecker bonds. These involved a questionable deal whereby about $15 million worth of bonds had been issued by French financiers in favor of Miguel Miramon, Juarez's rival. The claim was debatable, but with typical honesty Juarez had offered his country's payment of $750,000, which the Miramon faction had actually received in money. He then negotiated a settlement of British claims. Spain chose to remove her troops from Mexico and shifted them to the revolt in Santo Domingo.

But France used the dubious "Jecker matter" as an excuse for a major armed invasion of Mexico.

Napoleon III ordered his combat forces landed at Veracruz and instructed his commander of the invasion that he could expect to stay indefinitely so that "Mexicans who preferred a strong government" might have one. He later added that the French Empire proposed to limit the United States' extension to the south and also keep it from "controlling" the commerce of the Gulf of Mexico and the Caribbean.

Again a less-than-stable Mexico fought bravely against a strong and ruthless invasion force, and again it lost. During 1863, while the United States Civil War was at a critical climax, French forces captured Mexico City. On the Emperor's orders and at bayonet point, a makeshift "Assembly of Notables" was set up. Obviously without any widespread popular consent the captors maneuvered the assembly's "election" of Archduke Maximilian of Austria as Napoleon III's handpicked Emperor of Mexico.

The princeling and his girl wife, Carlotta, arrived the following year and, under direction of the French military, tried to establish the would-be "American Empire." Meanwhile the Confederate States of America made an unsuccessful proposal for an alliance with the Juarez government which held the status of a "patriots' government." Next the Confederate envoys sought an alliance with Spain whereby the Confederacy might gain dominance over the Gulf of Mexico. This move also failed in its object.

In September 1863, following the Union armies victories at Gettysburg and Vicksburg, Lincoln's secretary of state protested very strongly the French-directed maneuvers. Salmon P. Chase, the secretary of the treasury, spoke even more strongly for a "potent resurrection of the Monroe Doctrine." It was common knowledge that both of the cabinet members were speaking for Abraham Lincoln.

Their voices carried far. By then the Union armies were undeniably winning the Civil War, having developed what many saw as one of the most formidable fighting forces known to history. The United States House of Representatives passed unanimously a resolution of displeasure at the French actions in Mexico and refused to recognize any "monarchical government in the Americas . . . under the auspices of any European power."

Sulkily and on increasing pressure from the United States, Napoleon III began withdrawing the French occupation forces which were keeping the Maximilian Empire alive. The Mexican people as a whole had never approved the takeover; Juarez's patriots' government had lived on. Following the Confederacy's surrender in April 1865, General U. S. Grant, the victorious Union commander, was ordered to lead an army of 100,000 selected combat troops to the Mexican border; General Grant later stated that he "assumed that his mission would be to chase the French out of Mexico."

In Paris, meanwhile, John Bigelow, the ambassador to France, was advising Napoleon III that the United States definitely regarded any effort to "establish permanently a foreign and imperial government in Mexico as disallowable. . . ." During April 1866 the unhappy French Emperor ordered the withdrawal of all remaining French forces from Mexico. The flimsy, so-called Maximilian Empire fell like a house built of cards. Despite his personal charm and undeniable bravery, the Hapsburg prince was captured and executed by the patriots' government of Juarez, which resumed control of the country.

There were other evidences that the Monroe Doctrine could and would survive. Without violating its principles, the United States in 1867 succeeded in purchasing from Russia the vastness of Alaska and the Aleutian Islands for a mere $7.2 million—less than two cents an acre. The continent was thereby freed of another hold of empire. During the same year, by an act of the British Parliament, the British colonies of North America were made the Dominion of Canada, a great and soon to be friendly neighbor to the north.

6. Water Between Waters

ABRAHAM LINCOLN'S REVIVAL of the Monroe Doctrine led to a strong renewal of interest in what many regarded as the United States' one really usable foreign policy guide. Pan-American interest in the building of an interoceanic canal for the benefit of the Western Hemisphere increased, but the final choice of a building site had not yet been made. Some believed that Nicaragua offered the best canal route or choice of routes; others held with the Isthmus of Panama. The second issue awaiting decision concerned which country or countries would effect or supervise the building and which should safeguard or supervise the canal when it was completed. The United States was eager to take on the huge job, but for a variety of reasons several of the Latin American countries opposed this. Many believed that assigning the construction to an international business corporation would come closer to compliance with the intent or spirit of the Monroe Doctrine than would the assumption of responsibility by one country—such as the United States.

This argument, or point of view, found a strong supporter in the person of a flamboyant French engineer and promoter, Ferdinand de Lesseps, who had gained world renown as designer-builder of the Suez Canal, which was completed and opened to shipping in 1869. De Lesseps insisted that he fully approved of and sought to sustain and honor the Monroe Doctrine. He saw and publicized the building of an interoceanic canal in lower Central America as a bonanza for both hemispheric and world trade, and as an unrivaled opportunity for all nations of the Americas to gain practical and common benefit from what he termed the working spirit of the Monroe Doctrine.

De Lesseps virtually demanded that he and an international development company which he proposed to organize and lead be allowed to perform the task. Accordingly, and with carefree disregard of all the earlier treaties or agreements, the ever-enthusiastic "Builder of Suez" set about organizing the International Oceanic Canal Company for building an "American Suez."

At Bogota he readily gained official permission of Colombia to construct and operate a major shipping canal across that country's Isthmus of Panama. De Lesseps paused only long enough to reiterate that the Panamanian route was the best and that the project was entirely in keeping with the text and spirit of the Monroe Doctrine and the "admirable American principle of a private company serving international public good." Official Washington did not entirely agree. But it had a great deal else on its collective mind, including a long and painful business depression that followed the Civil War. Also, the public interest of the United States in Latin America was being shifted to and concentrated in Spain's principal island colony. Cuba's long struggles to gain liberation from

Spain were revived; American reactions were strongly in favor of Cuba and against Spain.

Well aware of this, General Grant, on becoming president, noted the rising importance of Cuba not only to the United States but to the Western Hemisphere at large. The geographical position of the "Pearl of the Antilles" was a most strategic one in terms of shipping throughout the Caribbean and the Gulf of Mexico and related to the defense of a transoceanic canal in Central America. Grant openly favored the outright purchase of Cuba by the United States, but Spain firmly refused. Grant then recommended that what he termed a more practical interpretation be made of the Monroe Doctrine. This included the use of the "policy" to improve trade with the other Americas, and more directly in keeping with the text, to keep Spain from reconquering the island in the event the revolutionary efforts won.

"More practical interpretation" certainly meant the advancement and use of the Isthmian Canal on which the De Lesseps company was already hard at work. But the undertaking was turning out to be far more difficult than De Lesseps and his engineers had expected. The progress was disappointingly slow—in great part because the labor force began suffering serious epidemics of malaria, yellow fever and other tropical diseases. After ten tragic years the canal-building sagged to a halt with less than a third completed.

Farther south revolts and civil strife were troubling many areas of Latin America. The most serious strife began in 1879 when Chile declared war on Peru and Bolivia, seized the rich nitrate beds along Bolivia's Pacific Coast, and captured Lima, the historic and beautiful Peruvian

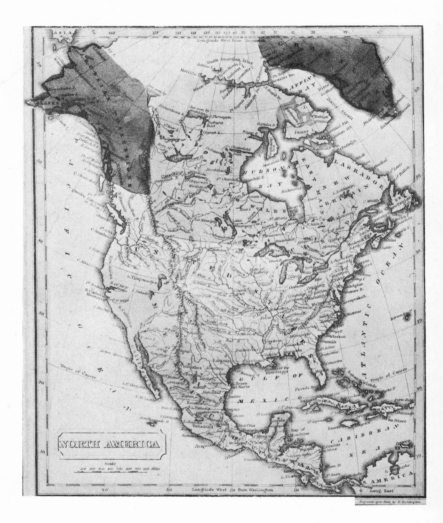

Map of North America. From an S. G. Goodrich Atlas of 1830.

capital. The United States government sought to arbitrate and bring the disturbing war to an end. The efforts were not a complete success, but they indicated the great value of the Monroe Doctrine as an instrument of peace— without undue interference in the internal affairs of fellow American countries.

Even so, what Grant hopefully termed warm Pan-Americanism was cooling. De Lesseps' failure to build a canal had proved disappointing to many shipping firms and had influenced more American trade to go directly to Europe. This, of course, served to cool inter-American relations and caused several Latin American governments to charge that the United States was deliberately neglecting their hoped-for commercial developments and using the Monroe Doctrine only as an excuse for meddling in their affairs without really helping them.

The so-called practical interpretation of the Doctrine was left increasingly in doubt. During the 1890s the blunt-spoken and determined President Grover Cleveland used the "Monroe attitude" to strongly protest British and German business moves in Venezuela and Mexico. A more successful use of the Doctrine was in settling a boundary dispute between Venezuela and the British colony of Guiana by means of neutral arbitration. British officials insisted that the Monroe Doctrine had no legal value as such, and could not be regarded as a code of international law insofar as it was merely a policy guide adopted by only one country.

Shortly thereafter a young and brilliant United States senator from Massachusetts, Henry Cabot Lodge, pronounced that the Monroe Doctrine is indeed a law—"it is of the great law of self-preservation, and should be so used by American nations and, as need be, others. . . ."

But many respected American newspapers, including several in Latin American capitals, took the common position that the Doctrine by then had outlived its usefulness; they argued that the Americas as a whole were already on a natural course toward making themselves independent republics. A much-cited proof was that during 1891 Brazil, in land area the largest of all Latin American nations, had changed itself from a kingdom to a federal republic markedly similar to the United States.

Many American newspapers and commentators were also pointing out that the "natural course" was also being demonstrated by Cuba, whose people were again joining in a common effort to free themselves from Spain. But the Cuban people were very badly divided in their quest for liberation. Many of the landholders and other wealthier citizens were siding with Spain, and many Cubans were therefore fighting other Cubans.

Official Washington was understandably confused as to how the Monroe Doctrine could be applied in such a situation. One suggestion was to resume efforts to buy the colony. Another, no doubt more in keeping with the Doctrine, was to try to persuade Spain to voluntarily withdraw her occupation forces and thereby give the Cubans a better chance to solve their social and group differences. As soon as that objective could be attained, Spain could be rewarded by way of business enterprises, such as sugar mills and railroads, which United States business firms would be permitted to build and operate with the understanding that the Spanish government would receive a share of the profits. Many United States business firms were showing interest in investing in and profiting from sugar, timber, cattle, tobacco, port operations, and other resources of fertile but badly managed Cuba.

President William McKinley, who entered the White House in March 1897, sought to steer a neutral course, yet at the same time use diplomatic pressures to persuade Spain to liberate her best New World colony. He seemed to be making progress as a peaceful persuader when a most baffling tragedy occurred.

Late in 1897 the light battleship the U.S.S. *Maine* was ordered to pay a friendly visit to Havana, where the handsome little battleship was cordially received by both Spanish and Cuban authorities. Then on the fifteenth of the following February the *Maine* became the victim of a still unsolved sabotage. It was blown asunder while at anchor, and 266 of its ship's company were killed. The reactions in the United States were so highly emotional that even though the guilt was not established, the outbreak of war with Spain seemed inevitable.

Some scholars still believe that the Spanish-American War was actually begun prior to the formal declaration of war against Spain by a congressional resolution enacted April 25, 1898. Several days before the declaration, the United States Navy's Asiatic Squadron had been battle-readied in its Hong Kong base and was en route under battle orders to Manila Bay. The decisive naval battle for Corregidor, the key defense of the Philippines, then the bulwark of Spain's Pacific empire, was won by the United States Navy before the war was a week old. The ensuing two-hemispheres war was fierce, but at least in Cuba it was mercifully brief, lasting only four months and twenty-seven days. In the Philippines, however, the belligerent aftermaths lasted more than three years and were felt throughout many Pacific lands.

Many observers, particularly in Latin America and Europe, held that the Spanish-American War violated the spirit and the accepted text of the Monroe Doctrine. Many insisted that it was essentially a war of conquest, aimed at making the United States a two-hemisphere empire and had little or no relationship to the desire of Cubans or other subject peoples to attain national independence.

Although not without some degree of factual support, this contention was not the entire story. The long-time concern and sympathy of the United States public for the Cuban people was unquestionably sincere, as was the long-prevailing desire of a majority of the Cuban people for independence.

This was not precisely the case in the Philippines. There the citizen groups had fought effectively against Spanish occupation troops and had already proved that their majority wished to break free of Spain. They would shortly oppose the takeover by United States forces with equal or greater vigor. The Philippine people simply did not wish to be taken over, even temporarily, as colonials of any power. The United States' acquisition of Wake, Midway, Guam, and other Pacific Islands formerly held by Spain was openly in violation of the Monroe Doctrine. And the so-called friendly annexation of the Hawaiian Islands, although it involved no violence, was not easy to justify in terms of the spirit and principles of that great document and frame of mind. The islands' citizens were not given an opportunity to engage in a democratic vote or plebescites to approve or disapprove of their rather abrupt annexations or so-called protective status imposed by the United States.

However, the applicability to Cuba was much more convincing. Before declaring war against Spain, the Congress of the United States had enacted the Teller Resolution, clearly stating that Cuba would not be annexed by the United States, which would presently accredit its status as an independent nation. The implied "period of protection" was effected, but self-sovereignty was presently granted the soon-to-be Republic of Cuba.

The United States' annexation of Puerto Rico, another Spanish colony, although peaceful, was again difficult to justify in terms of the Monroe Doctrine. Here again the citizens of the colony were not permitted a plebescite until after the takeover had been effected. Furthermore, the Puerto Rican people did not, and, as yet, have not received active representation in the U. S. Congress (Puerto Rican representatives may "sit" in the Congress, but are not permitted to vote on legislation.)

Monroe had foreseen that his "message" would necessarily have to be readapted and interpreted in terms of changing times and needs. He may well have foreseen that most presidents who succeeded him would try according to their own lights to reweigh and restate the Doctrine.

One of the most outspoken was McKinley's youthful vice president, who stepped into the presidency following McKinley's assassination in 1901. Theodore Roosevelt was an especially ardent advocate of what he construed the Doctrine to be:

> The Monroe Doctrine should be the cardinal feature of all the nations of the two Americas as it is to the United States. . . . It is not intended as hostile to any nation in the Old World. Still less is it intended to give cover to any aggression by one New World power at the expense of any other. It is simply a step, and a long step, toward assuring the peace of the world by securing the possibility of permanent peace in this Hemisphere. . . .

Our youngest president also noted that the Monroe Doctrine lived on as "a state of mind." Although it was not a law, it had attracted and won followings among lawyers, many of them world renowned. Many eminent Latin Americans were numbered among its most scholarly advocates. By 1900 these included Carlos Calvo, Brazil's world-influencing authority on internationalism, and Argentina's brilliant foreign minister Luis M. Drago. The two agreed that the Monroe Doctrine can never be applied merely by means of military might or other show of power and that by its very nature the Doctrine cannot impose mastery or infer the superiority of one nation or race over another. In essence it can only express the will of all people to live in freedom and support the rights of others to do likewise.

7. The Trial Renewed

During the 1890s the urge to use the Monroe Doctrine as a guideline and justifier for business development grew more conspicuous. One of the first and ablest advocates of this point of view, which would presently be branded "Dollar Diplomacy," was John Hay, President McKinley's secretary of state. Hay was also among those who felt strongly and deeply that completing a great international canal would be the best proof of the practical worth of the Doctrine. Accordingly, the gifted secretary took the lead in persuading the British government to give up its treaty rights to take part in building and managing the long-awaited project.

Britain graciously bowed out by yielding her treaty rights, but there were still many unsolved problems. Most of the experts agreed with the aging canal genius Ferdinand De Lesseps that the Isthmus of Panama route was the best. But Colombia did not wish to grant permission solely to the United States.

During 1903, after the government at Bogota had rejected another offer from the United States, a small uprising, which some called a revolution, took place in Panama. There had been earlier and similar protests in that area against the Colombian government, but this time a citizens' mass meeting at Panama City declared the Colombian province an independent republic.

Theodore Roosevelt hurriedly maneuvered his country's recognition of the hemisphere's youngest republic. Within a month the United States Senate approved a treaty whereby the United States would build the canal, take sovereignty over a trans-Isthmus land strip ten miles wide, pay Panama $10 million for the rights, plus an annual rental of $250,000, and reimburse the De Lesseps Company $40 million. In those times these sums of money were very large.

Ten years later, in 1914, the opening of the Panama Canal marked what many regarded as the greatest achievement in the history of transportation. Theodore Roosevelt orated that the great canal was "justified by the interests of collective civilization."

But was it justified by the Monroe Doctrine? At least part of the answer depended on whether or not the Panama "revolution" had been a good-faith expression of the will of the people of that province—without undue pressure or managing from without. If so, the recognition of Panama and the canal-building treaties were in keeping with the Doctrine; if not, the Doctrine had again been abused and shamed according to the sharp-tongued adage: "Whatever U.S. foreign policy is or isn't, it *has to be* labeled 'Monroe Doctrine.'"

The certain answer is not known and probably never will be. Even so, the concept and the completion of the Panama Canal would be mentioned in many history texts as working proof of the Monroe Doctrine in a "practical" and peaceful way.

8. The Great Divide

By 1914 the Monroe Doctrine had passed its ninetieth birthday. It remained one of the most quoted and admired documents and philosophies of internationalism. In terms of actual use its scores ranged from excellent to deplorable or needlessly bad. There was very good evidence that the Doctrine had served to protect some, possibly all, of the American countries from invasion or other forms of takeover by non-American countries. But this was offset by the proved fact that the United States, where the Doctrine originated, had done more than any other power to violate or misuse it.

The completion of the Panama Canal and the outbreak of World War I marked 1914 as one of the most decisive years in American history. It also put the Monroe Doctrine to several severe tests. The presidency of William Howard Taft (1909-1913) had been marred by bad relations between the United States and several Central American and Caribbean countries, particularly Nicaragua. Taft stood strongly with politically favored banking and other business interests in the United States. In several instances he was angrily and correctly accused of meddling or permitting others to meddle in the internal affairs of American nations that were at peace with the United States. On the whole the Taft years went badly for the Monroe Doctrine.

The next presidential administration, that of Woodrow Wilson (1913-1921), spoke more of the Monroe Doctrine, but used it as a groundwork for a policy of protectionism toward Latin America. Doctrine, of course, means "that which is taught or set forth for acceptance or belief." But the Wilson acceptance was that the huge and ever-growing strength of the United States should be used to steer, or if need be drag along, the weaker American states. This so-called protectionism caused many of the less strong American neighbors to feel that they were being treated as irresponsible children for the benefit of the *Yanquis.*

President Wilson had pledged that the United States would never again seize so much as one square foot of Latin American territory. But he entered the highest office with the erroneous assumption that all Latin American countries require and desire governments exactly like that of the United States.

This, of course, is one of the most unfortunate assumptions that the United States keeps on making—always mistakenly. Whether or not stated openly, the "Wilson Policy" was one of making what it termed "friendly protectorates" of American neighbor nations that could or would not "act exactly like we do." The "protectivism" (Wilson delighted in inventing or reshaping words such as "okay" and "normalcy") included the Taft-like "dollar diplomacy," which embraced such vagaries as using the U.S. Army and Navy as bill collectors for private interests, impounding the customs revenues of neighbor nations for the benefit of private as well as public creditors, and so on and on.

The *New York Times* and other respected newspapers were quick to point out that the Wilson administration was "carrying dollar diplomacy a long step further." The ridiculous invasion of Mexican territory in the tragicomic pursuit of alleged bandits (we had plenty of our own), and the stationing of U.S. Marines in Nicaragua, Honduras, Haiti, and the Dominican Republic, though all were at peace with the United States, were serious infringements of the Monroe Doctrine as well as of sincere neighborliness. By actual count the first "Wilson year," 1913-1914, was marked by nineteen violations of the Doctrine, more than had ever before been committed in a single year. With wistful sarcasm, the great Kansan editorialist, William Allen White, echoed that "all the little brown brothers ought always to be and act exactly like us. . . . That will make them practically perfect and very, very peachy. . . ."

The year that marked the official opening of the Panama Canal also saw the beginning in Europe of the First World War, in which the United States and much of Latin America would presently be engulfed. The Monroe Doctrine again seemed to be dying; it was being throttled and choked by a rampant multitude of overt violations. Through these years the plain, brave words of the plain, brave James Monroe echoed in vain:

> We have never taken any part in European wars and politics, nor does it comport with our policy to do so. . . . Our policy has been, and remains, not to interfere with the internal concerns of Europe. . . .

The great Doctrine was being cast aside like a worn-out sock. Could it ever be mended and used again?

The answer seemed to be lost in the deadly din of the greatest war the world had ever known. The Conference of Paris and another Treaty of Versailles that closed the almost global conflict and opened the way for a second and even deadlier one seemed hopelessly alien to Monroe's noble preachments.

Even so, several areas of the treaty showed the influence of the historic American doctrine. This was particularly true of the covenant of the League of Nations which echoed both the text and spirit of the Monroe Doctrine. Although the United States Senate refused to ratify the covenant, and the United States declined to join the League of Nations, the covenant also showed many recognizable hues, hints, and borrowings from Monroe's great message. This was in keeping with one of the last statements of Theodore Roosevelt: "Every well-meaning nation should itself become the sponsor and guarantor of the [Monroe] Doctrine; and its relations with those of other guarantors should be those of equality. . . ."

As the League of Nations fumbled along with sometimes noble intentions, but flabby muscles and a deluge of words, a brilliant American onlooker undertook to update the Doctrine. Charles Evans Hughes, President Hoover's secretary of state, sought to reestablish "Monroeism" as "Pan-Americanism." He received encouragement from the culturally oriented Pan-American Union and from his president, who set forth the "Good Neighbor Policy," which his successor, Franklin Delano Roosevelt, eagerly adopted.

Secretary Hughes' defense of the Monroe Doctrine received warm-hearted support from Latin America. The

Central American countries offered to open their admirable Court of International Justice to all the Americas. Chile's great jurist and scholar, Don Alejandro Alvarez, proposed entering the Monroe Doctrine in a master code of inter-American laws.

In more and more American capitals, advocates of world peace began to recommend the thoughtful reinstatement of the Monroe Doctrine as an all-Western Hemisphere instrument for peace. The United States Congress, and particularly the Senate, showed the urge to avoid further entanglements in European affairs.

Charles Evans Hughes presented to the American Bar Association what he termed an updated Monroe Doctrine. This emphasized that the "Monroe Doctrine for the Twentieth Century" (1) is still primarily a policy of self-defense; (2) is still the guiding light of United States foreign policy; (3) does not and must not infringe upon the independence and sovereignty of other American states; and (4) although still an instrument for peaceful cooperation among all nations, must yield to inevitable revisions to meet changing needs. Finally, the twentieth century confronts the United States with "rights and duties" not listed in the original, such as seeking to remedy "unsettled conditions in certain Caribbean countries," "our friendly advisor's relations with Cuba," and the "temporary military governments" established by the United States in Haiti and the Dominican Republic "to prevent anarchy—i.e., the collapse of all government."

Secretary Hughes insisted that the Monroe Doctrine is timeless in principle but requires updating as a "practical commandment." He pointed out that Monroe had accepted the truth that no nation can live wholly apart from other nations. But Monroe could not foresee how completely the twentieth century would bring all nations into one community and do away with "truly distant places."

Hughes saw the Monroe Doctrine as a very important background document for foreign policy and for supporting national legislation. But the baffling 1920s found the Monroe Doctrine being quietly shelved or benched in official Washington, D.C. There were no impressive diplomatic advantages or practical inter-American attainments, such as the Panama Canal building, to encourage its return to public attention. As the decade ended, President Hoover came forward with a recommended "Good Neighbor Policy," which was enlightened and recognizably in the mood of the great Monroe's message. But infringements by the United States, such as stationing armed Marines in nearby Latin American countries that were at peace with us, were not corrected. United States business concerns continued to reach into Latin America and in great part to shape their own rules or maintain a lack of rules. By or before 1930 the slowly improving inter-American trade began to slacken as it encountered a worldwide economic depression. On the whole there seemed to be no immediate or widespread urge to restore or even refer to the Monroe Doctrine.

In March 1933 the presidency of Franklin Delano Roosevelt opened promisingly in terms of Pan-American relations; in most Latin American capitals "F.D.R." was soon accepted as a symbol of better neighborliness throughout the hemisphere. Roosevelt did not sponsor so-called dollar diplomacy. Furthermore, his administration began withdrawing the Marines from their unjustified assignments to countries in Central America and the Caribbean and to free the Republic of Cuba from authorized meddling or "protection" by the United States. Although it was not mentioned openly, the Monroe Doctrine was being freed from its more bothersome shackles and permitted to stand and walk again.

But the 1930s presently began to feel the cold shadows of a gathering hot war that would darken both hemispheres. Because many Latin American governments were actually in closer touch with European capitols than was Washington, D.C., the gathering shadows were first noticed more widely south of the Rio Grande than north.

By the mid-1930s one could also hear more mention of the Monroe Doctrine in Latin America than in the United States. It was comforting to know that the Doctrine as a frame of mind definitely remained alive in the Americas to the south.

But the threat of war continued to spread and darken and defy. The peacemakers were not inheriting the earth. Roosevelt's foreign policy shifted to a war policy, to making the United States "the arsenal of democracy." Various Latin American peace policies arose bravely, but vast brute force was rising even more rapidly, as the totalitarianism of Nazism spread over more and more of Europe.

World War II swept over most of the earth like an unmanageable and all-destroying hurricane. The principles of peaceful diplomacy, religions, and other great directives of peace seemed to be facing total destruction.

But some would rise again. The resurrections would include at least the more basic principles of the Monroe Doctrine. However much beaten, battered, and neglected, this uniquely American gospel had not perished utterly. The "frame of mind" showed clearly in the various armistices and peace treaties that sought to mark the end of the global war, and in the charter of the United Nations.

World War II brought the Americas into the world community. This served to accentuate the need to uphold principles of respect for national integrity, the right of peoples and nations to choose and maintain their preferred forms of government and to live in and with their chosen bodies politic, all basic elements of the Monroe "frame of mind." Also accepted was the fact that such a live-and-let-live philosophy cannot be restricted to one hemisphere. The United States had emerged as the number one world power. The Americas were of one world; the pledge of not "interfering with the internal concerns of the European powers" could no longer be limited to Europe. The range and reach of the most distinctive American directive of foreign policy could not be thwarted or limited.

However, in notable instances they were thwarted; in others they were beclouded with complicating technicalities. A very serious lapse occurred during the Truman administration, which authorized and instituted U.S. military intervention in the internal and domestic concerns of an ancient but ever-changing Asiatic nation, Korea. The flagrant contradiction of the principles and spirit of the Monroe Doctrine was further accentuated by the onset of a war by presidential decree and/or orders, in violation of the Constitution of the United States, which specifically directs that only the Congress has the authority to declare war. The contention that the United States was taking the militant action as a member of the United Nations and by authority of the Security Council thereof could not erase or bypass the fact that the prolonged and bloody war was waged without a lawful declaration by the Congress of the United States. The scope of violations of the Monroe Doctrine was further enhanced by the commonly accepted fact that as of that time the United States substantially dominated the United Nations.

Certainly the Monroe Doctrine would never sanction warfare against and military invasion of any nation for the willful purpose of overthrowing or aggressively interfering with its popularly chosen form of government, however unattractive that form of government may be to the government of the United States. Belligerent support or defense of a newly established or claimant government involves an exacting and often extremely difficult adjudgment as to whether or not the new or claimant government actually represents the will or free choice of a majority of its citizens. In this very demanding area of necessary knowledge, the United States, like many other powers, has shown a repeated tendency to substitute inference or prejudiced emotionalism for valid facts.

Regardless of its professed objective of damming the spread of "Communism," the ensuing Korean War unquestionably smudged the integrity of the Monroe Doctrine, and, to borrow one of Monroe's many homely but expressive phrases, "warp and over-crowd its type frames."

Throughout the tragic conflict, as before and after it, the applicability of the great frame of mind to United States relations with the other Americas was being further tarnished by the so-called foreign aid programs. These provided a seemingly unending showering of U.S. Treasury monies on frequently ill-chosen political favorites or factions, including obnoxious military dictatorships, throughout most of Latin America. In instance after instance the "aid" did not truly benefit—failing to filter to or otherwise reach those who genuinely needed it. Even more regrettably, in many instances the military aid has served to maintain in office or continuing power incompetent or ruthless dictators or strong-armed tyrants whom a countable majority of citizens do not wish to follow or see perpetuated in office.

Here again, and through the crowding years, one hears the calm, reasoning voice of James Monroe: "The true policy of the United States is to leave the new states . . . to their own devices of government. . . ."

The multiply tragic Korean War ended in a befuddled cease-fire which could only prove again that just as there cannot be a truly good war, there cannot be a truly bad peace. Still open to debate was how much and how directly the Monroe Doctrine had been defiled and contradicted by the Korean War.

During the Eisenhower administration the Monroe Doctrine was permitted to show occasional glimmers of life. At the very least the violations by the United States were less calamitous than they had been during the Truman administration.

However, late in the 1950s the violations list began to gain an especially distressing addition. This was the less than open but very real participation of the Soviet Union in a bold and partly successful attempt to support and exploit the takeover of Cuba by the Fidel Castro regime.

Whether or not what is sometimes termed the Castro Revolution was the will and choice of a majority of the Cuban people is not known for sure, at least not to this writer. In any case, the right or privilege of any nation to effect a change in its own government was never denied by the Monroe Doctrine; indeed, it was and is surely supported. But the direct and willful entry of the Soviet Union into Cuban affairs was undeniably what Monroe had cited and specifically anticipated as an attempt of a foreign power to extend an alien political system "not acceptable to the States south of us" to the independent Republic of Cuba. In Monroe's own words, "We shall consider any attempt by European powers to oppose or control in any other manner the free States of the Americas as an act unfriendly to the United States. . . ."

The anguish of Cuba waits unrelieved. Within less than a hundred miles of the United States a leading Eurasian power had willfully violated the Monroe Doctrine. But so, alas, had the United States in Korea. Just as two wrongs cannot make a right, the multiple violations of a guiding doctrine cannot sustain that doctrine.

The violation of Cuba by the Soviet Union was destined to continue. But so, no less deplorably were the United States' presidential violations of the Monroe Doctrine and the Constitution of the United States. The arbitrary and militant moves of the United States to control the destinies of Asian nations, specifically Vietnam and, in general, Indochina, from without and within by resort to war could well utterly destroy the Monroe Doctrine.

Unquestionably the overextended nightmare of the Indochina-Vietnam war, the longest in our national history and perhaps the most contradictory to our principles and heritage of integrity, has marked the most prolonged and deplorable violation of the Monroe Doctrine—both of its text and of its spirit.

The crucial question here is: Is the Monroe Doctrine still alive? Or has this great American instrument of justice, this frame of mind for hemispheric and worldwide neighborliness, been destroyed completely?

The first answer is a definite yes; the second is a no less definite no.

Nobody can deny that the Monroe Doctrine has been

The New York Times.

© 1960, by The New York Times Company.
Times Square, New York 36, N.Y.

LATE CITY EDITION

U.S. Weather Bureau Report (Page D-3) today.
Mostly fair, warm and humid today.
Partly cloudy, less humid tomorrow.
Temp. range: 84—72; yesterday: 83.7—67.6.
Temp.-Hum. index: high 70's; yesterday: 77.

VOL. CIX. No. 37,426.

NEW YORK, WEDNESDAY, JULY 13, 1960.

16 cents and 26-mile zone from New York City stamps on Long Island. Higher in air delivery cities.

FIVE CENTS

PLATFORM WINS AFTER CLASHES ON CIVIL RIGHTS

SOUTH THE LOSER

Democrats Pledge to End Discrimination —Ask Big Budget

Platform, Page 20; South's report, 21; Collins talk, 19.

By W. H. LAWRENCE
Special to The New York Times.

LOS ANGELES, July 12—The Democratic National Convention overrode Southern protests tonight to adopt a "big-budget" platform that included the strongest civil-rights plank in party history.

CONGO URGES U.S. TO SEND TROOPS; PLEA IS REJECTED

Mutiny Continues as Tension Mounts—Whites in Flight Across All Borders

By The Associated Press.

LEOPOLDVILLE, the Congo, July 12 — The nation that emerged to replace Belgium's mid-African colonial empire twelve days ago asked today for United States and Belgian troops to keep the country together.

JOHNSON STRIVES TO HALT KENNEDY

They Meet in a TV 'Debate'
—Texan Criticizes Rival

PLANE NOT OVER SOVIET, U.S. SAYS, DECLARING ATTACKS MUST CEASE; RUSSIA DEFIES MONROE DOCTRINE

CUBA SUPPORTED

Khrushchev Vows Aid in Any Move Against Guantanamo Base

Transcript of Premier's news conference, Pages 6 and 7.

By SEYMOUR TOPPING
Special to The New York Times.

MOSCOW, July 12—Premier Khrushchev contended today that the Monroe Doctrine was dead and promised to back up Cuba in any effort to get rid of the United States naval base at Guantanamo Bay.

SHARP NOTE SENT

Washington Declares RB-47 Victim of a Wanton Assault

Text of United States note is printed on Page 7.

By WILLIAM J. JORDEN
Special to The New York Times.

WASHINGTON, July 12—The United States Government sent a strongly worded note to Moscow today charging that Soviet fighter planes "wantonly attacked" an American plane over international waters July 1.

used very badly—in greatest part by the very nation which almost a century and a half ago accepted it and resolved to accredit it.

Yet on occasions, including very important occasions, the United States has cherished and honored the Doctrine and used it for international good.

This, too, can happen again and again and again. For the Monroe Doctrine is actually neither dead nor doomed. It lives as an enlightened frame of mind, as a gospel or glad tiding, as a way shower for peace and justice for all nations.

PART II

FOR
DISCUSSION

9. What if There Had Been No Monroe Doctrine?

If there had been no Monroe Doctrine, our country and the Western Hemisphere as a whole would almost certainly be very different from what they are now. Chances are the differences would not have been for the better.

Very probably, South America would have been, indeed might still be, a continent of colonies of one kind or another. Perhaps these would be called dominions or protectorates or spheres of influence or bloc members. But whatever the label, they would be essentially colonies, even if not wholly within the British dictionary definition of a colony as "a region with a responsible government, whether or not it has an elected legislature."

A reasonable supposition holds that had it not been for the Monroe Doctrine, Latin America at large, both mainlands and habitable islands, would have kept or skidded back into the status of colonies or dependent states, either controlled or strongly influenced by governments beyond their national boundaries.

Indeed, South America might have been doomed to be the Africa of the Western Hemisphere, an open range for colony-hunters. The Caribbean Sea might have been militarily used as the New World Mediterranean, with its principal islands and more strategic shorelands outfitted as sea and air bases, bulwarks for offensive as well as defensive warfare.

Had it not been for the Monroe Doctrine, the maps of the Americas, including the United States, would be markedly different. The chances are that our own country would be much smaller than it is. Quite probably neither the Oregon Territory nor California would now be in the United States. There is a distinct possibility that Alaska would have remained a property or colony of czarist Russia, and in due course of the U.S.S.R. The odds are that our Northwest and Pacific states would now be either British "protectorates," or an extension of the Dominion of Canada. The western boundary of our country would perhaps be in the eastern fringes of the Rocky Mountains. However, our southern boundary might cut deeply into what is now Mexico.

If there had not been a Monroe Doctrine, the odds are that we would still be speaking and writing English—"American English"—but this, as at present, would be largely limited to North America above Mexico, where French might now be the official language. As in present-day Africa the traveler in Latin America would probably be hearing tribal or other "old native" tongues intermingled with French, German, Italian, Dutch, and perhaps others, but with Spanish and Portuguese only minor entries.

To better envision what the Western Hemisphere might have become had there been no Monroe Doctrine, let us look again and more closely at what the Americas were like as the President's extraordinary annual message was being read on December 2, 1823.

The United States was still a rather loose union of twenty-four states: Maine, recently separated from Massachusetts, and still sparsely peopled Indiana were typical of the then "brand new" frontier states. As already noted, the estimated census of the United States was about 11.5 million—somewhat less than the present census of Pennsylvania. At least four-fifths, some believe closer to five-sixths, of our people lived on farms or in rural communities or very small villages. There were barely a dozen interstate roads, none of them paved. There were still no effective railroads or telegraph lines or telephones. Three short, inland canals were open or under construction, but most travel was by ships or small boats on rivers and lakes, or on coastal shipping lanes. As Monroe had noted, the foremost American recreation was "staying to home."

New York, Pennsylvania, and Virginia were the three largest states, each with somewhat more than one million people. The two Carolinas, Ohio, Massachusetts, and Kentucky had somewhat more than a half million people each. Although its combined census was less than a fifth of the total, New England was being listed as the "beehive of American population."

About three-fourths of the people of the United States still lived in the Atlantic states, from Maine through Georgia. Ohio was the pivotal western state; it had more people than all its neighbors combined; Indiana had only 137,000; Illinois, 55,000; Missouri, 66,000, and so on downward.

The United States as a whole was still not far advanced from a frontier state as far as comforts of life were concerned. Among the many evidences of this was the preponderance of log houses with few or small windows. (Glass and nails were still the most expensive building materials.) Clothing for men, women, and children alike was home-sewn and in great part home-woven. Long hair was in vogue, partly because few could afford barber services. (Many American males wore their hair in braids; the elderly and the bald who were vain frequently or usually wore wigs.)

The United States had no big cities; Philadelphia, then the largest, had about 166,000 people, who held licenses for a most impressive total of 1,197 buggies, wagons, or other "rigs," all drawn by horses, mules, donkeys, or cattle (oxen). Washington, D.C., was commonly described as a backwoods town lost in the mud and to the mosquitoes. The western boundaries of the United States were vaguely described as the Rocky Mountains. Such were some of the measures of the senior American republic which had so courageously accepted the Monroe Doctrine —to honor, revere, and enforce.

The remainder of North America included the United States of Mexico with perhaps 3 million people, and about half again as much land as it now has; the wilderness-and-jungle federation of Central America, with a combined census guessed at 100,000; the British colony of Belize, with perhaps 50,000 people, and the little known and be-jungled narrows of Panama, a frontier province of New Granada (Colombia), reportedly with fewer than 1,000 people. The "larger half" of North America was still held or claimed by Great Britain, in all about 3.6 million square miles reaching from the "Canada Pacific" through the present Canadian province of Quebec and including the "Maritime Colonies" of New Brunswick and Nova Scotia; and to the far north, the Hudson's Bay Company's "Great North Country." The total population of British North America was being guessed as one million.

Czarist Russia's America was based on Alaska, but as noted, still included about a third of a million additional square miles of claimed lands.

While the Monroe Doctrine was being born, almost two-thirds, or at least 22 million, of the New World's population, were Latin Americans. These included the far-scattered, largely mountain- or highland-dwelling publics of eight countries that had recently declared their independence. These were the actual or hoped-for acceptors of the Monroe Doctrine. As Monroe had noted, the population of the United States was divided into threes: a third white and free, a third slave (principally black), and a third "noncitizen" (including indentured or bonded servants, newly arrived immigrants, Indians, and "rovers"). As of 1823 an estimated 85 percent of all Latin Americans were Indian or part-Indian; eight to ten percent were Negroes; the remainder were European immigrants, in greatest part Spaniards. Such were the backgrounds of the Monroe Doctine's first constituents.

Latin America of 1823 also had groups or units of colonial possessions, including those held by Great Britain, Spain, France, the Netherlands, Denmark, and Sweden. Most were small, and many were no more than colonial trading posts; all were acknowledged as permissible by the Monroe Doctrine.

As a public servant of the United States, with long experience, Monroe had learned a great deal about early nineteenth-century colonialism, and he had found much of what he had learned discouraging and deplorable. In European capitals, particularly those of Great Britain, France, and Spain, he had noted that colonies, like other properties, were being seized, bought, sold, swapped, held and earned from, or disposed of for the benefit of favored

Map of South America. From an S. G. Goodrich Atlas of 1830.

individuals or companies and for the profit or other advantage of empires. Some colonies were valuable only because of strategic location (for example, Gibraltar), or as shipping bases (the Azores), or for superior harbor sites (Hong Kong), or as control points for favored fishing waters (Nova Scotia or the Falkland Islands). But most were being sought for their readily marketable resources and to provide balance or other advantages to other colonial holdings of a given empire.

Monroe had noted that the motives for taking colonies were centered on what he called the magnets of wealth—rich ores, furs and pelts, ivory and other natural harvests such as fine timbers and palm oils, or highly profitable crops such as cotton, spices, and natural dyes.

The Americas were naturally endowed with all these existent or attainable sources of colonial wealth. Monroe was keenly aware that the industrial revolution, by then gaining mightily in the British Isles and throughout much of Europe, was multiplying demands for all industrial metals, particularly the richer ores of iron, lead, zinc, copper, and the precious metals, led by gold; and for fiber crops, especially cotton, flax (for linen), and wool. Commercial fishing and whaling were important throughout most of Europe; and as never before, Old World fishing fleets were thriving in many different New World waters. During the Napoleonic wars the fur trade had grown enormously. The demand for furs continued to grow as Russia, Sweden, Prussia, and other cold-country powers garbed their armies in fur cloaks and capes.

The motives for seeking and seizing colonies also included the use of native labor that could be had for coolie or "peon" wages or could be enslaved or "contracted for" at comparatively tiny costs. The procedures for acquiring colonies were freeing the empires of many risks and expenses. These included the politically favored colonizing companies, which richly rewarded their shareholders while exploiting a given territory and presently returning it to the Crown as an addition to the empire. Nobody could doubt that the Americas abounded with desirable lands and resources.

Monroe had reflected that colonialism as an institution "bore precious little of charity or the milk of human kindness." He had noted that in building colonies the native populations were rarely valued as more than slave or quasi-slave laborers. He had observed that as "colony keeping" grew more profitable, it was tending to become more brutal. He repeatedly quoted a cynical British colonial secretary who had stated: "We rarely whip or mutilate our native territorials; where required we leave those disciplines to other natives."

The observant Monroe noted that as colonialism grew materially, it dwindled morally, a falling from grace with "an ever loudening thud." In short, the author of the Monroe Doctrine saw little good in colonialism as it prevailed in 1823. He recognized that although some of the colony sites in the Americas had been taken without great violence, most had been and several were being held by means of military establishments—by what Monroe termed "the hard spine of the bared sword, the loaded musket and the cannon." He was convinced that the best American protection against European colonization was the continued formation of independent American states.

But this acceptance again conflicted with the need to protect the independent countries. Old Soldier Monroe knew that most of Europe was at least temporarily winded and gasping from the real-life nightmares of the Napoleonic wars. Even so, the principal powers were again building or at very least planning bigger armies and navies and making them available for taking, supplying, and otherwise holding additional overseas colonies. Even badly troubled Spain was known to have about 16,000 soldiers stationed in Cuba, then her most promising New World colony; that was more than twice the entire enlistment in the "regular army" of the United States in 1823.

The aging president was well aware that the "frame of mind" he hoped his countrymen would accept as a permanent international policy of the United States posed very real hazards. It carried the open promise that the United States would stand against any European power or powers that might seize, or conspire to seize, additional territories in the Americas or seek to return the newly independent countries to colonial status. Monroe did not deny that what he termed the "key text" of his message might have to be, in his words, "backed up with bared swords, loaded muskets, and fighting ships," as John Calhoun, his secretary of war, had so grimly confirmed.

He believed, and clearly he was willing to gamble that no major colonizing power would open a major war of conquest for colonies in the 1820s. But he hesitated to predict that this would be assured for the 1830s. There are few absolute certainties in international affairs.

As Commander-in-Chief of the Army and Navy, Monroe also knew that his country was not prepared for a major war. Indeed, the widely scattered and undersized United States Army had been suffering painful strains and aches from General Andrew Jackson's "brushes" with Florida Indians. Monroe detested Indian fighting and had tried hard to squelch it; he had also tried to keep up at least a nucleus of a defensive army. But his country was still very short of treasury funds. As Monroe had stated, every dollar looked as big as the moon and wasn't much easier to lay hands on.

The United States Navy of 1823 was not easy to measure by present-day yardsticks. Necessarily it was made up entirely of sailing craft, mostly small, highly maneuverable, lightly gunned ships suited to speedy attack and quick getaway. The roster of forty-six fighting ships still included fourteen Cape Cod-type schooners, two-masters rated between 80 and 140 tons; seven sloops (three- or four-masted and slender-hulled to enhance speed), a like number of heavier but somewhat slower "brigs" or brigantines (blockier vessels that were square-rigged on the foremasts and fore-and-aft rigged on the mainmasts to make the more operable in close quarters).

There were several corvettes, heavily besailed and speedy vessels with tiers of guns, and a remnant of frigates —larger than corvettes and more heavily gunned but less maneuverable. The Navy also had a "filler" of sailed transport craft. The United States had won her narrow victory in the War of 1812 principally at sea and on the Greak Lakes particularly Lake Champlain, but Monroe knew that at best the United States Navy of 1823 was no match for any major combat fleet of any principal European power.

Furthermore, in his determination to endorse his administration's legislation against the slave trade, Monroe had authorized assigning most—at least two-thirds—of the available fighting ships to patrolling against slavers' ships and slave stockades all the way from the African coasts to the Caribbean. There was no doubt that the Navy was well manned and courageous, but in terms of combat numbers and firepower instantly available for fighting off a strong invasion fleet anywhere in the American Hemisphere, it did not qualify.

From experience Monroe had a high regard for the volunteer land forces of the United States as defenders of their homeland. While secretary of war he had followed the frequently remarkable victories of volunteer militia units that were self-equipped, led by civilian officers elected by volunteer common soldiers, and in many instances supplied and paid by their home communities or townships. He had eagerly looked on while rented ships and contract crews won decisive clashes on the Great Lakes and elsewhere.

He had profound confidence in the American's willingness to make his own individual stand for freedom. Correctly, he sensed this same quality of devotion and courage in Latin Americans, but he could not help knowing that most of Latin America was even more handicapped by poverty and remoteness than his own country. The peoples' armies that had succeeded or helped in gaining their countries' independence had already faded into civilian life. As yet no Latin American country had an effective navy.

At least in private Monroe had granted that none of the new Latin American countries could be counted on to beat off a determined attack by any principal European power. He could and did count on the United States to offer "spirited discouragement" to any invasion effort. This spirited discouragement could serve, however, only as a "balance of decision" for preventing European powers from seizing American territory. The very special annual message had developed all the foregoing. It had shown Monroe as a deeply believing man, a quietly bold man, and a resolute gambler.

Portrait of James Monroe by Rembrandt Peale, painted in the White House during the period 1817-25. Now on exhibit in the James Monroe Law Office and Memorial Library, Fredericksburg, Virginia.

"We owe it therefore to candor, and to the amicable relations existing between the United States and those powers, [Russia, Prussia and Austria] to declare that we should consider any attempt on their part to extend their system to any portion of this Hemisphere, as dangerous to our peace and safety. With the existing Colonies or Dependencies of any European Power we have not interfered, and shall not interfere. But with the Governments [the South American Republics] who have declared their Independence, and maintained it, and whose Independence we have, on great consideration, and on just principles, acknowledged, we could not view any interposition for the purpose of oppressing them, or controuling in any other manner their destiny, by any European power, in any other light than as the manifestation of an unfriendly disposition toward the United States."

Excerpt from the original draft of President James Monroe's annual message to the Congress of the United States, December 2, 1823. Courtesy James Monroe Memorial Library, University of Virginia.

10. The Lands
Were Coveted

In 1823 most observers believed that Czarist Russia and Imperial Spain were then the most serious threat to American liberties. In his message to the Congress Monroe flatly stated that Spain was not able to take back her former American colonies by force or otherwise. In private the fifth president doubted that, despite angry-sounding *"ukases,"* Russia and her czars would resort to war to extend the boundaries of Russian North America. He recalled the gypsy chief who held that gypsies do not kidnap other people's children because they have more than enough of their own. Monroe believed that "those Russias" already had more homeland than they could begin to use.

As he knew, Russia was concentrating her military efforts on holding or gaining Baltic frontiers. Since the 1770s, the czarist government had been recruiting European peoples, particularly from Prussia and what would presently be the German Empire, to help colonize the Russia's Georgia and the vast spaces of Siberia. During the 1780s and 90s Czarina Catherine II had renewed the recruiting of settlers, and the Russian government was still seeking more people rather than more lands. Monroe also knew that Russia's "Arctic American Colony" (Alaska) was doing poorly; it had not yet developed even one prosperous town or seaport.

The observant Monroe personally regarded Great Britain, France, Prussia, and perhaps the Netherlands as the colonizing powers that bore the closest watching. Britain was then the most rapidly growing empire; her merchant fleets were multiplying and her navy was being rated as invincible. France was reverting to her earlier position as a colony-taking empire with strong business interests in favor of "expansionism." The Netherlands, too, was not wholly out of the running as a colonizing power. In the course of his championship of the then Commonwealth of Liberia, the free-slave settlement in tropical Africa, Monroe had learned that great Africa was an especially tempting quarry for colonizing powers—both the oldtimers and the newcomers. After Africa they would very likely look to South America.

The Western Hemisphere abounded in what Monroe termed coveted lands. His awareness of this was of course the prime motive of his special message. But his belief that fate and geography, as well as developing events, were on the side of the Doctrine was firm. Never before on two adjoining continents had so many independent countries come into being during a single lifetime (the American Revolution had begun only forty-seven years earlier). Undeniably the new American countries were being born of the desires of the majority of the so-called common people.

Monroe, who came of "common people," was confident that the century of the common man had already begun and that it would presently sweep over most or all the earth. He therefore felt that fate and God were on the side of independent nations capable of, as he put it, "standing in the sun and throwing shadows."

But the aging and most popular American president also recognized that the growing dissatisfaction of the common people of Europe with their harsh, selfish monarchs might serve to encourage the seizures of additional overseas colonies. These could provide additional havens of escape for those who were unhappy in their homelands. The overseas colonies could also provide more wealth for the reigning governments, and some little part of this wealth might even seep through to the poor people at home.

Monroe's thinking had supplied a great deal of helpful revelation. He had called attention to and clarified the writing on the wall which told that all nations, or bodies politic, like the people in them, are not and cannot be exactly alike.

This fact of life is basic to the philosophy of the Monroe Doctrine. The independence of nations is a vital need, frequently or usually an absolute condition of their survival. Throughout the world of 1823, particularly the Western world, many people—from professional statesmen and career public servants to everyday citizens who could not be branded as revolutionaries—were becoming aware that a government that is good for one nation is not necessarily good for all nations. A colonial or other subservient government, or an old or classic government that cannot be fitted to the real and changing needs of real and changing people simply cannot be good enough.

This acceptance is implicit in the Monroe Doctrine, and it caused the Doctrine, or "frame of mind," to win widespread notice throughout Europe as well as the

Americas. In time many other countries would attempt to devise their own versions of the Monroe Doctrine, but without notable success.

As Monroe sensed and as history has confirmed, the Doctrine, both as a frame of mind and as a hallmark of understanding foreign policy, was a distinctive American creation that came at a most propitious time in a nation best positioned to accept and cherish it. Thus, from its birth to the present time the Monroe Doctrine remains uniquely American. Its global applicability does not change this truth but only accentuates it.

But what if there had been no Monroe Doctrine?

11. The Probables
and the Possibles

GRANTING THAT ONE can only guess what the Americas would now be had there been no Monroe Doctrine, one is not obliged to guess blindly. There are rational likelihoods that are clearly aligned, in some instances solidly foundationed by history. The fact that one must necessarily resort to such qualifying waivers as "probably" or "more than likely" or "it seems to me as if" does not erase the recognizable way-markers of known history or the reasonableness of studied guesses.

The first of these is that many, quite probably most, of the American nations long recognized as independent would now be colonial holdings of older nations, or, as in present-day Africa, former colonies only beginning to find new lives as independent nations. Otherwise our Latin American neighbors might not be called colonies; that now unpopular word has been largely replaced by such terms as "dominion" (which indicates equal status of citizenship and at least partial self-government, and a state of being "united by a common allegiance to a crown"), or "trust territory," or "protectorate." However, with colonies as

with canned goods and political parties, a change of name
does not necessarily change the contents.

Monroe had recognized that colonies rise, ebb, or
otherwise change with the empires to which they belong or
have belonged. Because of this very evident fact of life,
he did not see Spain's former New World colonies as being
in resurrection. Rather, he saw the Spanish empire as a
sort of museum of geographical antiques including desert
fringes, such as the Sahara; and of remote, jungle-strewn
shorelands, such as Spanish Guinea in Africa; and potentially valuable island colonies, such as Cuba, which was
not "proving out" as a successful colony. Shortly before
his death in 1831, James Monroe, on hearing that the
Spanish emperor, Ferdinand VII, had named his year-
old daughter Isabella as his successor, commented wryly
that the royal infant could hardly do worse by the empire
than her father had.

Monroe's estimate of the second European colony-
taker in the New World—Portugal—paralleled his view of
Spain. He recalled that Portugal's claim to Brazil, the
largest state of South America, dated back to 1494—only
two years after Columbus's historic voyage. By 1500 Portugal had laid claim to huge Brazil, but by 1557 (with the
death of her strongest king, John III), Portugal had passed
her high mark of wealth and power. By Monroe's time
Portugal was a poor little country being wagged by a poor
big empire. At the time the Monroe Doctrine was first
submitted, Portugal still bled from the Napoleonic wars
and was heavily dependent upon her strongest ally, Great
Britain. Nobody could seriously expect that Portugal would
attempt to retake Brazil or other extensive American territories.

Monroe had predicted correctly that the American

"ambitions" of czarist Russia were less than invincible. The final proof would not be forthcoming until 1867—forty-four years after the first airing of the Monroe Doctrine—when Russia sold her Alaskan territories to the United States at a price clearly suggesting that the most solid things about them were the ice and perennial tundra.

Sweden and Denmark held Caribbean islands as token colonies—as some feared, seed for much larger colonies. Monroe had not shared that fear or concern. Interestingly, he referred to the Scandinavian countries as the "Kalmars." (In earlier times Sweden, Norway, and Denmark were fellow members of the Union of Kalmar. But in time quarrels and warfare between the Danes and Swedes had broken up the union; Sweden triumphed and came forth as an independent nation with Gustavus as her monarch.)

As Sweden grew and fought for a place as the first power of the Baltic Sea, her colonizing ambitions became centered on holding that advantage. However, in the early eighteenth century Peter the Great of Russia succeeded in making his country the undeniable first power of the Baltic.

The maximal colonizing centuries, the eighteenth and nineteenth, found Sweden and her Scandinavian neighbors heavily involved in European wars, including wars between themselves.

In his letters dated between 1820 and 1825 Monroe had noted only four powers, Great Britain, France, the Netherlands, and Prussia, which he regarded as likely claimants or takers of additional colonial holdings in the New World. Had there been no Monroe Doctrine, the number of "suspects" might have been at least doubled.

The most probable offender was France. The France

of 1823 and the ensuing half-century was definitely not
La Belle France that had so valiantly aided the cause of
the British-American colonies in the Revolution. Nor was
she the impoverished, missionary-sponsoring empire-seeker
of the early sixteenth century. "New France," which had
once included or claimed the upper half of North America
—all lands and inland waters above a line projected from
the present site of Philadelphia to the Pacific—had been
mapped and pioneered by an amazingly gifted, profoundly
religious Catholic layman, Samuel de Champlain. Champlain had proved himself one of the most compassionate
as well as able of all the great colony-builders.

But his humility and acceptance of cause above money
were not to endure. By the time of Louis XIV (1638-1715)
France was moving strongly into place as a foremost colonial power. New France had been supplemented by
much of India, and the beginnings of wealth—yielding
colonies in Eastern Asia and the nearer South Pacific as
well as strategic island holdings in the Caribbean and the
seeker of a foothold in South America.

But during the eighteenth century luck went against
France. The Seven Years War, known in the Americas
as the French and Indian Wars (there were actually two
of them), resulted in France's loss to Great Britain of
most of India, all of French North America, and other
forfeitures which reduced France to a second-rate power—
also to the so-called era of beggary which opened the
way for the French Revolution. The epochal storming of
the Bastille (July 14, 1789) brought France a recess from
colonizing, but it did not actually throttle French ambitions for rebuilding a mighty overseas empire.

This fact was dramatically demonstrated during the
1790s by the meteoric rise of the Corsica-born Napoleon

Bonaparte, who had already shone brightly as one of the more able and popular generals of the French Revolutionary Wars. During the two ensuing decades the Napoleonic wars roared along and hoisted France back into place as the first power of Europe—until July 1815, when Napoleon and his last-fling army went down to final defeat by Britain at Waterloo.

But France's lust for colonies had not waned. Monroe watched with deep interest her new ruler, Louis Phillippe, called "The Citizen King," whom he personally knew and liked. Seventeen years after Monroe's death another and markedly different Louis took the leadership of France (in 1848). Four years later this German-schooled nephew of Napoleon Bonaparte proclaimed himself Napoleon III, King-Emperor of France.

The third Napoleon was aggressively colony-minded. This fact is noteworthy because it would shortly reveal some of the higher and lower politics of colony grabbing and empire building, and some of its typical motivations.

Napoleon III stood for and with wealth-building and the imperialism it invited or demanded. On the other hand, he could not overlook the fact that liberal groups were again gaining strength in France. Paris had remained a world capital of clashing philosophies and democratic and antidemocratic moods.

The public reaction to colonialism was also mixed. Particularly in North Africa, sturdy French farmers were pioneering ably. Other French colonies, such as those in Asia, ranging from remnants of French India to what is now called Indochina, and farther, were measurably thriving.

The lesser Napoleon was using colonial developments to win the approval and support of French bankers, manufacturers, and foreign traders. To better the progress, he courted and won British favor by joining in an alliance which presently led to Anglo-French victory and Russian defeat in the Crimean War. With the other hand he maneuvered to restore his image as a champion of liberty by supporting Sardinia in the Italian War of Liberation against Austria.

Meanwhile, the plump, grim nephew of the first Napoleon was searching various horizons for colony possibilities. He recognized Mexico, badly torn by revolutions and other civil strife, as a tempting prospect. He had been assured that Mexico was among the richest of nations in mineral wealth. French manufacturing needed industrial metals; the French government needed gold. The location of Mexico was favorable in terms of Western Hemisphere trade development.

We have already noted the highlights of France's unsuccessful intrusion into Mexico; the military fronting for an "empire" that France hoped to control by way of a transplanted puppet emperor; a crafty exploitation of the anguishing Civil War which temporarily preoccupied the United States. The intentions were ominous; the procedures were fairly typical of the then obtaining intrigues for colonial expansion and/or profitable domination.

The specific overtures were hardly less ominous. Great Britain had accorded at least a gesture of approval by supplying a naval escort at Veracruz for French invasion forces; Spanish troops had actually joined in the invasion, until abruptly withdrawn to quell a reported revolt in Puerto Rico. Prussia, meanwhile, had shown evidence of joining the gangster "play." Prussia's already powerful Otto von Bismarck, who enjoyed making a kind of parlor game of outwitting the overweight French emperor, had reportedly established an agreement whereby if France would stay neutral while Prussia walloped Austria, Prussia would reward France with "territorial cooperation." If that boded good for France, as Napoleon III assumed, it was certainly no blessing to Mexico or the hardly less vulnerable Americas to the south.

The dismal failure of the Maximilian coup was unquestionably due to bad timing and faulty intelligence (including overestimating the Confederate chances of winning the Civil War and underestimating the competence of Benito Juarez, the patriot president of Mexico).

But the outcome was not inevitable. The colony grab, or behind-curtains takeover of Mexico by imperial France, could have succeeded. Its chances would have been much stronger had there not been a Monroe Doctrine. Whatever her name, Mexico could have become France-in-America, a way station for more and bigger takeovers in Latin America—by European-based empires.

12. Britain Might Not Have Waived the Rule

GREAT BRITAIN'S GESTURES of approval of the French invasion of Mexico had not gone unnoticed. The British Empire was also growing lustily. Without the "frame of mind" inherent in the Monroe Doctrine, Great Britain might well have taken the chance of provoking another war with the United States as a more or less inevitable consequence of the aggressive resumption of colonizing the Western Hemisphere. In land area British North America remained substantially larger than the United States. In terms of monetary returns Britain's North American colonies (the British Parliament had not yet declared Canada a dominion) were still short of being a bonanza. But the self-liberated American colonies that became the United States had been no great bargain. Most of the time, His Majesty's exchequer had lost money on them.

The nineteenth century found Britain in superb position to make a growing, wealth-promising American empire still bigger and much more profitable. Britain ruled the waves and more and more of the lands. In Europe she held such strategic keys as the Channel Islands, Gi-

121

braltar, and Malta. In Asia her colonial spreads included most of India, Malaya, Ceylon, and anchor points such as Singapore and Hong Kong. In the Pacific the multiplying empire was seining in scores of land possessions, including wild Australia, more readily developable New Zealand, and the far-flung "British Pacific Islands," to mention only the headliners. The vastness of Africa, the earth's second largest continent, already doomed to become a colonial grab bag, was being opened to other distinctly promising British holdings, the Union of South Africa, Rhodesia, Kenya, Uganda, Gambia, Tanganyika, Nigeria, the Gold Coast, Sierra Leone (the first free-slave colony), and so on into the still dark but beautiful continent.

To say that Great Britain desired no more American colonies would have been much like saying that a typical millionaire doesn't wish to take home another dollar or shilling. Her Majesty's empire was notably lacking balance or showing in Latin America. The crown colony of Jamaica had turned out to be a profitable colonial base, but Jamaica is small (about the size of Connecticut), and charming as many of them are, the other British Indies are even tinier. (Queen-Empress Victoria termed the British West Indies and British Honduras as only "pretty dots in a beautiful sea.")

British Guiana in mainland South America had turned out to be another kind of American colony takeover—not in violation of the Monroe Doctrine. Dutch ship men had first claimed the territory for the Netherlands and Dutch emigrés had settled there as early as 1610. Later, English settlers came into this tropical wilderness and just before the American Revolution, English privateers forceably seized the territory. But the British government soon restored the jungle wonderlands to the Netherlands, and, in 1814, following the first downfall of Napoleon Bonaparte, managed to win the portion called British Guiana as a treaty plum.

This demonstrated the easier way to win or acquire colonies. But it did not solve the obvious imbalance and limitations of the British holdings in the southern half of the Western Hemisphere.

In 1831 Britain made her Guiana lands a crown colony, thereby opening the way for more of the same. But the next British move—to purchase Cuba from Spain —did not succeed. History had already proved that taking colonies by force or by antics of power politics was usually easier and cheaper than buying them.

No clairvoyance was needed to see that drastic British expansion in the Caribbean or Central America could have severely strained relations with the United States, even if there had been no Monroe Doctrine. The less risky course and the more abundant pickings were much farther south and west. Here were possibilities for persuading young republics to accept British "protection" in return for much wanted and needed developments which Britain was in a position to offer.

Although British relations with Buenos Aires, or Argentina, were less than cordial, this new and amazingly fertile frontier country was still only feebly governed and cripplingly isolated. Attractive bargaining points included three basic facilities that Argentina most urgently required and British industries and investors were in the best position to supply. These were merchant shipping, including riverboat lines; railroads; and bank credit. Britain could supply all three.

A still more accessible and more immediately rewarding area for British entry into lower South America would

have been Chile. British citizens, including adventurous
Irishmen, had already settled in numbers and built friendships in that new republic; indeed, many had valuably
aided the Chilean struggles for independence, and English
shippers and former navy personnel had also aided that
cause. As a result, Chile was distinctly pro-British, and the
trading world was already finding out that Chile had much
to give. Its rich and readily takable mineral resources included the principal metals—for England's multiplying industries, and vast quantities of nitrates for the thinning
soils of England.

Chile's neighbors to the north were also enticing.
The earlier relationships between Chile and Peru (which
included what is now Bolivia) were less than cordial, but
this invited British skills for arbitrating native quarrels
and misunderstandings while persuading new countries
to merge into what were called trust territories.

British relations with the Perus were also good; there
were visible chances to develop a major British colonial
holding in lower and central Pacific South America. Con-
ceivably and in time this might have formed a partly
self-governing dominion of the mineral-rich Andean states.
Again the British capabilities for providing shipping, railroads, and credit might well have been effective persuad-
ers, particularly so if there had been no Monroe Doctrine. Quite possibly such a Golden Horn of South America could have been extended to include the wonderfully
rich soils and near-perfect agricultural climate of what is
now Ecuador as well as in time, Colombia and all the
Guianas. The total might have eventually made up the
British Dominion of South America.

13. The Germani

At the College of William and Mary, James Monroe had studied and remembered the *Gallic Wars* and other writings of the Caesar Julius. His later letters make several mentions of the stalwart people whom Caesar called the "Germani."

As a statesman and presently as a chief of state, Monroe differentiated between the kingdoms of Prussia and Austria, and the total numbers of the Germanic people. He liked and respected the latter. He had never especially liked the imperial governments of Prussia and Austria or, for that matter, Russia—the Big Three of the so-called Holy Alliance, which he detested.

The German Empire as such did not come into being until 1871, forty years after Monroe's death. But the influence of the Germanic peoples as a whole on the Americas was well begun more than a century before Monroe's birth.

Until late in the nineteenth century the *Germani* had contributed to most of the Western world by means of emigration. They had taken useful places throughout Europe and in many American colonies, beginning with

Pennsylvania, New York, and Georgia. At the time of the American Revolution a probable tenth of the people of what would be the United States were of German descent. By the Civil War this proportion had about doubled. By 1900 nearly a fourth of the United States population was of German descent; by 1910 our country had about 2.5 million German immigrants, about 8 million second-generation German-Americans, with perhaps 15 million more of German descent.

Meanwhile, German immigrants had been pouring into the other Americas, particularly Brazil, Argentina, Mexico, and Venezuela, as well as Canada. The *Germani* were exceptionally good settlers and developers; "German-Brazilians" and "German-Venezuelans" excelled in establishing farms, plantations, stores, banks, factories, boat lines, schools, clinics, and many other useful enterprises. In great part the Germans married native peoples or earlier immigrants, raised integrated families, and built lasting friendships—without seeking to found colonies in the formal sense of the term.

This began changing in the 1870s with Prussia's crushing defeat of France's Napoleon III and his so-called Second French Empire. The capture of Paris signaled the beginnings of what old-fashioned history books termed German nationalism. With the Prussian William Hohenzollern as her emperor, the German Empire made up of four kingdoms, twenty-five states, eighteen duchies (or dukedoms), and three formerly free cities came into being and began taking a place as a colonizing power. In 1884 the "Iron Chancellor," Otto von Bismarck, maneuvered for a German protectorate over a large area of Southwest Africa. With the help of the Karl Peters' Company and other government-chartered companies which served to pioneer colonies, Germany joined the grand grab for central Africa and took over a first Oriental pivot, Kiao Chao, on the China coast.

In 1888 the colonizing tempo increased when William II became emperor. With the support of a powerful army and a greatly strengthened navy and merchant marine, Germany moved still more aggressively into Africa, China, and the South Pacific. As German relations with both Great Britain and the United States cooled, her interest in Latin America warmed. The basis for these relations was the successful German immigration in those countries and the high regard in which most of the immigrants were held. As before, the Imperial German government also counted on its "children" in the United States to keep peaceful relationships. A near quarrel developed during the middle 1890s when the German government censured the Venezuelan government for permitting alleged mistreatment of German nationals in Venezuela. Berlin appealed in vain to Washington, D.C., for corrective action.

This spat served as a raised-voice reminder that official Germany had never regarded the Monroe Doctrine as valid; again and again, important German leaders had spoken scornfully of it. Bismarck, for one, had called the Doctrine "that American pretense." Adolph Wagner called it an "empty threat." William II had called it a hallmark for a dangerous "pushing people." Prominent German policy-makers, such as Helmuth von Moltke and Albrecht von Roon had joined in citing the Monroe Doctrine as a "pompous cover up for its sponsor's own violations."

There were many other indications that, without a Monroe Doctrine, the thrust of Germany's colony-taking might well have reached into Latin America. Had it not been for that "American pretense," the odds are that Imperial Germany might have taken substantial colonies without penalty of war with the United States. Certainly what was then the great and growing German Empire had gained possession of colonies and so-called trust territories for Germany by means short of war.

Meanwhile, German war capabilities had rapidly taken first place among the European powers, and by 1890 the new German navy was second only to Great Britain's.

This spelled power for taking and holding colonies. But a less militant strength endured in the hundreds of thousands of German settlers in at least seven countries of Latin America. Among the most effectively "Germanized" regions were the resources-rich southern states of Brazil, particularly Sao Paulo and Rio Grande do Sul (already known as "Germany-in-Brazil"), and Venezuela, where German bankers, traders, and other enterprisers were gaining influence.

Particularly in these areas, without the Monroe Doctrine to impede, the expanding German Empire might very well have developed colonies. Or by a more convenient course it could have claimed "protectorates" similar to those whereby Germany first entered Southwest Africa, a routine move whereby a strong country takes control of a weaker one allegedly to protect it from a worse fate. Another stock excuse for takeover could have been the claims of injuries, such as those made by German businesses in Venezuela, as a basis for "impounding" a nation's revenues. (The United States would presently be following a somewhat similar course in Nicaragua, Honduras, Haiti, and Liberia). With nations as with citizens, the control of essential income is one of the more effective means for depriving them of independence.

Another course might have been to encourage or support German-immigrant revolts or organized protests against existent governments in Latin America and rewarding with a so-called status of protection granted by the German Empire. The kaiser's government had used like tactics or stratagems for acquiring what presently became German-African colonies.

Whatever the maneuvers, had there not been a Monroe Doctrine the twentieth century might have seen a Germany-in-Brazil or a Germany-in-Venezuela.

14. Others who Might Have Come

MORE THAN TWO CENTURIES before Monroe was born the Netherlands was already busily colonizing the American Hemisphere. New Amsterdam, now New York, began as a Dutch colony. Farther south, other Netherlands adventures in New World colonizing would turn out to be more successful and much longer enduring. The Netherlands West Indies and Dutch Guiana (Surinam) on the South American mainland are now the best-known examples.

However, dissent within the homeland and participation in many costly European wars proved to be the hobble that retarded the Netherlands' colony-building in Latin America. In 1830, the year before Monroe's death, the people of the southern provinces of the Netherlands (descendants of the stalwart people whom Julius Caesar had called *Belgae*) revolted against the upper provinces, now Holland, and gained independence, and held it with the help of Britain and other European powers.

By 1840 Holland was again in position to look about for additional Latin American holdings; long before then she had acquired much know-how, wealth, and shipping from her more successful colonies, particularly the resourceful East Indies, now the Republic of Indonesia. Brazil's Atlantic wilderness province of Pernambuco could have been tempting, and without the Monroe Doctrine, might have provided effective sites for Dutch colonization in Latin America.

History did not work out that way. The colonizing dice would presently be cast differently for Holland's neighbor Belgium, which Great Britain continued to sponsor as a protected and so-called neutral power.

By 1865 Belgium began trying her hand and luck at colonizing. Her monarch, Leopold II, had exceptional talents as a businessman as well as in winning the support of his subjects. Since his country did not have either the wealth or shipping resources then required for an all-out plunge into colonizing, Leopold set out to develop a new approach. He began by having expert surveys made of areas then available. The best choice seemed to be a jungle-strewn area covering a million square miles of Equatorial Africa, south of French West Africa and west of Britain's Tanganyika. The Belgian monarch set up in Brussels the International Association for the Exploration and Civilization of Africa as a planning group. Next he sponsored the founding of the so-called Congo Free State.

"Free State" meant that the huge realm, including the earth's fourth-largest river, was declared open to all nations for purposes of "peaceful" trade, development, and travel on terms approved by the commission. The early responses were promising. Business firms and promoters from many nations sought and gained permission or concessions for mining, logging, river transportation, and various trading rights.

Surprisingly, in 1884, the United States was the first

power to officially recognize the Congo Free State. International business firms began to promote a similar plan whereby the king of Belgium would appoint another commission of experts to direct the formation of a "free state" in the inner Amazon Basin of Brazil, which in many respects is a vast tropical frontier not too different from the Congo. The Brazilian government listened without taking immediate action or position. Was the "free state" concept a means for developing great new tropical frontiers—short of routine colonization and therefore not contradictory of the tenets of the Monroe Doctrine?

The on-the-scene reports from the Congo experiment were less than reassuring; indeed, they were disappointing, even distressing. Journalists and other onlookers reported in lurid and heartrending detail that, commission or no, the Congo concessionaires were committing terrible wrongs, cruelly using Congolese workers, maneuvering warfare between tribes, using hired killers as "enforcers" and to wage brutal warfare against Arab tribes in the region.

Leopold hastily appointed another *comité* to investigate. He confirmed his willingness eventually to return the Free State to Belgium as a routine colony. Although the Belgian Parliament enacted laws aimed at "cleaning up the Congo," the image of enlightened colonization via international free states quickly vanished.

The pipe dreams (or possibly potential nightmares) of an Amazonian Free State also faded abruptly. Thus the possibility of a developmental colony with an empire as supervisor died stillborn. Many students of the subject saw the failure of the Congo Free State as an open admission that "enlightened" colony building could not be made a reality, that the colonial system was already self-doomed.

The belated efforts of Italy to build up a colonial empire served to support that view.

Italy's first parliament was convened and the reign of her first king (Victor Emmanuel) began in Turin just as the United States' Civil War was beginning. But the Italian Empire did not take form until 1885, with Eritrea, or Italian East Africa, the first principal colony. By 1890 Italy was playing the empire game vigorously, but was finding attractive colony sites hard to come by. There was evidence that the then youngest European empire was eyeing Latin America. Italy's emigrants had supplied their homeland with strong American ties and the New World with millions of very fine citizens.

To cite one especially noteworthy example: by 1900 an estimated 3 million Argentinians were Italian or of Italian descent; the capital, Buenos Aires, was being pointed to as "Rome in South America."

Had there not been a Monroe Doctrine and if South America had already been opened to European empires, Argentina or a substantial part of it might have been at least a protectorate of Italy—possibly a "balancer" of Italian Somaliland in East Africa.

Granting that two or more "ifs" do not make a certainty, Italy's desire to expand her overseas empire was quite evident. Following World War I, when the German colonies were taken over by the Allies (mostly Britain and France), Italy's interest in acquiring colonies was again very much alive. During the 1930s a Mussolini-led Fascist Italy opened a postseason colony hunt, again turning to Africa. The principal victim was the ancient kingdom of Ethiopia, but this ever-interesting nation was freed again by the fall of Fascism in 1944.

That story was a historic exception to a more general truth. The close of World War I had marked the beginning of the end of traditional colony-grabbing; The Americas were no longer colonial hunting grounds, at least along the lines of the older patterns.

In both hemispheres colonial peoples were growing more and more dissatisfied with second-rate or nonexistent citizenship. They were also beginning to demand that their "motherlands" provide them with more and better services —schools, roads, railroads, medical facilities, and so forth. The 1920s found colonialism growing much less profitable and much more difficult to keep intact.

World War II sounded the death knell for what had been known as Western imperialism. One after another the remaining European empires began striving to improve colonial relations and slackening the severity of controls. Most of the moves were too late to be effective. The British Empire merged into the British Commonwealth of Nations. Most of the French Empire sloughed away. Holland's once enormously profitable East Indies gained liberation as the Republic of Indonesia. Africa of the 1950s and early 60s set an all-time record by giving birth to sixteen new or would-be republics. Most of the former British American colonies were granted "peaceful sovereign status." Even the older and more reactionary colonial powers such as Spain and Portugal moved to liberalize the "controls." Even if tardy, these developments confirm John Quincy Adams's perhaps mystical conviction that in time European colonialism would somehow erase itself, or otherwise go away.

15. Present and Future

MONROE SUBMITTED AND believed ever so sincerely that the newer American "states" required and deserved the respect and good neighborliness of the United States and, occasionally, our protection from "interference" by any Old World power.

His goal of mutual and common benefit was plainly stated. "An attack on the other Americas must be defined as an attack on ourselves. . . . Presuming that they succeeded, they would extend to us. . . ."*

As we have already noted, the historic message to the Congress of the United States was specifically dated December 2, 1823. But its thinking and thesis were in no way attached to any calendar leaf. The reach and scope of its value have not been limited to any given year, decade, or century.

By his own admission, Monroe's message of December 2, 1823, was most concerned with the needs, problems, and dangers of the Americas together—the New World. But it clearly recognized the interdependence of

---

* This quotation, closely similar to the original text, is from the *National Intelligencer*, Washington, D.C., December 9, 1823.

the New World and the Old. The seizure or founding of American colonies by the European powers, or the act of forcing or otherwise causing American nations that had already declared themselves independent to return to the status of colonies was the most worrisome peril then current.

Although the president's message of 1823 did not recite in extensive detail the means or devices whereby Old World powers might interfere with the independent nations of the New World, it stressed the responsibility of the United States to defend, as needs required, the younger and weaker American "states."

Monroe did not hide his acceptance of the fact that positive actions might be required. He was well aware that the tides of empire were rising, that the Old World powers had increasing cause for seizing New World territories. For many years, both as an envoy abroad and as an elective official at home, Monroe had observed and pondered the various ways or devices for acquiring colonies, which he described as the "feeding troughs of the empires."

He noted that the prevailing "ways and means" included (1) armed invasion or other military violence; (2) the "implanting of false leaders"; (3) the takeover of independent states or territories by infiltration or by routine purchase or trading; (4) the willful weakening or destruction of native leadership, or (5) the maneuvered turning of tribe against tribe or race against race among resident peoples.

The elderly president, who liked to be called "Old Mr. America" or even "Old Mr. Cocked Hat" (this referred to his old-fashioned or, as some said, pre-Revolutionary dress), foresaw that the perils of the free nations to the south were varied and would remain so, inevitably changing with the times. Even while serving as Madison's secretary of state, he had clearly recognized numerous stumbling blocks or chug holes in the Pan-American roads to independence. He also recognized that the United States' indifference, or accentuation of convenience, or involvement with domestic problems could blunt the effectiveness of the Doctrine both as a way shower to good foreign policy or a moral commandment—his own phrase here was "tablet of good." His prime reliance was on a frame of mind which he deemed truly American and eligible for perpetuation.

There is considerable evidence that the fifth president would not have been too much surprised by what would presently come about as violations, deliberate and otherwise, by the United States government. He definitely foresaw the possibilities of serious strife between the United States and its next-door neighbor Mexico, but he hoped that this would be settled by means short of war or open violation of his Doctrine. But Monroe also foresaw and clearly indicated in many of his later letters that his countrymen would "generate" and prove the many attainable and enlightened uses of the frame of mind which in time would sparkle and allure like a river of diamonds.

As he had confidently foreseen, with the Monroe Doctrine, South America was *not* destined to be darkened by colonialism like a second Africa; the Caribbean would remain a free sea—not a foreign-controlled New World Mediterranean, and regrettable wars could and would be avoided. He could and did hope that because of the Doctrine no new colonies would be taken from or in the Americas and that no sovereign American nation would ever be reduced to colonial status.

Apparently Monroe did not foresee that in time, about

125 years from 1823, another kind of subservient state might appear in the American Hemisphere. This is the so-called satellite state, currently associated with the Soviet Union. "Satellite," of course, has come to mean a smaller body, such as the moon which follows and attends upon the gravity pull of a larger body, such as planet Earth. But the actual derivation of "satellite" is from *satelles*, the Latin for "guard."

The Soviet-engendered satellite is both a guard and a guarded state. It is a colony, at least to the extent of being under the control, or the decisive influence, of a parent country and/or ideology. To a degree it is also what the builders of the Roman Empire long ago termed the buffer state (or colony). "Buffer," as everyone knows, means a padding, a protector against hard blows or possible concussions. Thus a buffer state came to mean a country located between two or more larger powers that, because of the buffer, are less likely to make war on one another.

As World War II came to an end, the Soviet Union managed to set up in eastern Europe and beyond an impressive number of combination satellite and buffer states. This marked the revival of what is a new era or epoch of colonialism. Monroe was well acquainted with the use of the old-style, or "owned," colonies to extend empires from continent to continent and hemisphere to hemisphere. The empires of France, Britain, and Spain were then typical examples, but even then Monroe was more deeply concerned with what he termed the "territorial anticks" of Russia. He had long since observed that the foreign policy of the Russias (as he correctly called them) showed no real change as czar succeeded czar. Present-day historians now go a step further and point out that the foreign policy of the U.S.S.R. is remarkably similar to that of the czarist Russias.

In this connection, beginning as recently as the latter 1950s, all of us have been aware of the emergence of what is in effect an American satellite of the Soviet Union— within less than 100 miles of the mainland of the United States. This, of course, is the former Republic of Cuba, now officially renamed the Socialist Republic of Cuba.

Its sad and discomfitting story began taking shape during 1957-1958 when the beautiful and tragic island nation became the scene of still another citizens' revolt against an obviously corrupt and inadequate national government.

By 1958 an effective revolution force had gathered in the sugarcane and open-country province of Oriente. The exceptional leader was a then youthful legal scholar and son of a respected Spanish-immigrant, sugarcane planter in Oriente. Fidel Castro gained public notice as a rather eloquent young mystic who professed special devotion to the cause of the long and cruelly exploited poor people of Cuba. His followers and colleagues included young and ardent protesters from pretty much all over the island, and several immigrant Communists and professional agitators. In the beginning all professed that they were taking arms for the purpose of bringing about a free Cuba for all true Cubans.

But the professed goal was abruptly changed. By January 1, 1959, Fidel Castro and his diverse followers succeeded in establishing in Havana, and presently throughout Cuba, a political dictatorship. This led into the beginning of what Castro described as a five-year rule by decree —with Castro himself the "premier" and prime decreer.

On the following February 7, the vehement young

dictator appointed a president and council of ministers, all close colleagues, "to represent the sovereign power of the state." That accomplished, Castro extended his "authority" to govern by decree for an indefinite length of time.

With his brother Raul as chief of Cuba's armed forces and a bevy of self-admitted Communists in other key positions, Castro took the lead in establishing his own dominant political party, the United Party of Socialistic Revolutionaries, and directed the changing of Cuban courts to so-called revolutionary tribunals. The dictatorship controlled the press and other communications and instituted the seizure or expropriation of private properties, including lands, industrial plants, and many other business enterprises.

Drastic as it was, the Castro-led revolution, in its beginning, did not directly violate the text of the Monroe Doctrine or its principles as previously interpreted. But this, too, was abruptly changed on May 1, 1961, when Castro officially proclaimed that Cuba was and will remain a Marxist-Leninist socialist state.

This act spelled out the arbitrary imposition of a foreign political system on a previously sovereign American nation. Unlike the more recent changeover of Chile to a possible socialistic state by the public election of a socialist president and legislative majority, the "socialization" of Cuba was by arbitrary and dictatorial decree which the majority public was not given the opportunity to approve or disapprove.

Furthermore, the Castro ultimatum, which openly labeled the national government of Cuba as communistic, directly admitted a satellite-style relationship between Cuba and the Soviet Union.

The U.S.S.R. was already replacing the United States

as the principal provider of Cuba's foreign trade. As a next step a varied throng of Soviet government technicians swept into Cuba to take advisory or directional roles in the planning or management of the nation's agriculture, public housing, many of its industries, and various government functions, including housing, health, and school administration.

The "invasion" by Soviet technicians was and is not without beneficial results and, of itself, did not involve defiance of the Monroe Doctrine. But it served to further precipitate a situation in which the Castro government continued to strengthen economic and ideological ties with the Soviet Union, while the United States continued to react by placing embargoes or "no-goes" on most commercial exports to Cuba and by closing off the previous more or less friendly relations between the two countries.

The virtual certainty that the principles of the Monroe Doctrine were or would shortly be openly denied as a result of the Cuba-Soviet Union tie caused concern in official Washington. Beginning with an official notice of the U.S. State Department, dated July 14, 1960, both the Castro government and the Soviet Union were informed that the policy of the United States was and will remain one of "explicitly reaffirming the Monroe Doctrine." The Castro government evaded, while the Soviet government replied curtly and in effect that "the Monroe Doctrine is dead."*

Before the Castro government had weathered its first year, two basic facts were self-evident: Obviously the first

---

* The Khrushchev "pronouncement" dated September 11, 1960, and repeated in substance during 1961, 1962, 1963, was almost a carbon copy of the *ukase* of Czar Nicholas I, dated January 27, 1824.

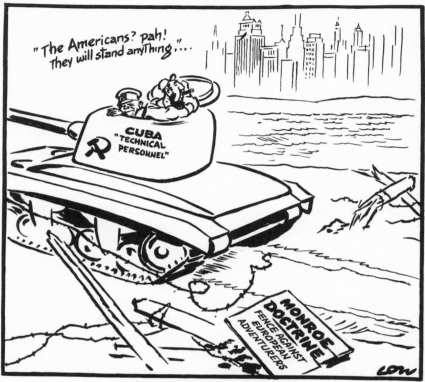

FAMOUS LAST WORDS

David Low cartoon reproduced by permission of the Trustees and the *London Evening Standard*.

was that the Castro assumption of power had never heeded the desires and civil rights of the majority of Cuban citizens. The other was the open evidence that the Castro regime was already aiding the Soviet Union in gaining a durable foothold at the very doorway of the United States.

By 1962 the perils that are part and parcel of Cuba's role as a Western satellite of the mightiest of Old World powers assumed still more disturbing shapes and involved more serious contradictions of the Monroe Doctrine. By then Soviet-directed construction and arming of atomic missile bases on Cuban lands were providing all Americans very real cause for alarm.

The administration of President John F. Kennedy confirmed surely and protested strongly the Cuban presence and arming of alien missile bases that were capable of severely damaging population centers in the United States or elsewhere in the Americas. The fact that Soviet technicians and military personnel were known to be establishing an attack base near the center of the American Hemisphere was giving the Monroe Doctrine a new and still bigger aura of importance.

Aware of this, President Kennedy and his administration increased the strength of protests and clearly indicated that the Doctrine was indeed alive and directional. Not all the ensuing moves by the United States were successful, as the tragic Bay of Pigs incident showed. But Kennedy's support of the Monroe Doctrine proved to be effective as well as admirable. Begrudgingly the Soviet leadership ordered the missile bases, at least the ones that had been surely identified by U.S. observers, dismantled and their warheads and other "destruction loads" removed from Cuba.

The too much battered, beaten, and otherwise abused frame of mind which is the Monroe Doctrine again won support. But this significant challenge told of even more crucial trials to come and of the profound need for further reweighing the great document and vetting it for future uses.

The compelling, indeed life-or-death, needs for the great Doctrine do not dwindle or fade away; rather they grow with every passing day. Comparably, the quandary and tragedy of Cuba, as a Soviet satellite near the heart of the American hemisphere, continues. During 1970, for example, there were reliable reports of Soviet moves to set up—with due permission of the Socialist Republic of Cuba—shore bases for atomic submarines.

Developments like these necessarily defy and negate the now historic principles and directions of the Monroe Doctrine. They also raise or stir profound questions regarding the justice and wisdom (in the light of that Doctrine) of the "world policing" practices of the United States.

Referred to here are our country's attack sites, or "defense bases," which include potentially highly destructive weaponry, in both hemispheres. Not all these establishments are as yet publicly revealed, but it is impossible to deny that many or most of these facilities are or could readily be made capable of the mass destruction of peoples and the grievous injury of governments or bodies politic that are not at war with the United States.

Too much of the military planning and prevailing military facilities of the United States are by their essences in contradiction or open defiance of the just, firm, and now traditional American frame of mind that lives on as the Monroe Doctrine. It is a noble and consistent doctrine; as such it deserves to be nobly and consistently sustained.

As this book is being written, the Nixon administration and its loyal opposition are joined in the openly stated acceptance of the Monroe Doctrine and the intention to sustain it as a basic document for shaping and, as necessary, revising our foreign policy. This position, as now taken and pledged by both of our senior political parties, offers heartening testimony that our political leaders are aware that the Monroe Doctrine is indeed a living issue, that it retains great usefulness, that it can be honored and sustained for the enduring benefit of all the Americas and the hard-tried world beyond.

"This [Monroe Doctrine] was of real truth in the beginning and real truth never dies."

The foregoing is another quotation from the author of Doctrine, the builder of its frame of mind, the foremost attainer of the Era of Good Feelings, and, by actual vote count, still the most popular president of the United States.

James Monroe believed, too, that history, particularly American history, does and must repeat itself.

Even in his own lifetime he believed ever so sincerely that the frame of mind that others chose to name the Monroe Doctrine was and would remain of living and valid American history. As such it could and would repeat itself. When bespattered, it would prove to be self-cleansing. When crushed to earth, it would rise again. When apparently dead, it would somehow effect its own surrection.

James Monroe was a believing man. His prime confidence was in God and in what he termed the common Americans, among whom he included himself. He commended usefulness, and he exalted trustworthy way-markers. To him the frame of mind others called the Monroe Doctrine was such a trustworthy way marker that it was for all "good people" to follow.

So the Monroe Doctrine lives on, challenging and usable, taking wondrous strength from yesterdays that clasp hands with tomorrow.

Additional Reading

JOHN QUINCY ADAMS. *The Lives of Madison and Monroe.* Buffalo: Thomas Jewett & Company, 1850.

STUART G. BROWN, ed. *The Autobiography of James Monroe.* Syracuse: Syracuse University Press, 1959.

W. R. CRESSON. *James Monroe.* Chapel Hill: The University of North Carolina Press, 1946.

D. Y. THOMAS. *One Hundred Years of the Monroe Doctrine.* New York: Macmillan, 1924.

LUCIUS WILMERDING. *James Monroe, Public Claimant.* New Brunswick: Rutgers University Press, 1960.

Index

DATE DUE

APR 10 '73			
APR 28 '73			
NO 21 '77			
DE 12 '77			
AP 15 '78			
DE 19 '78			
FEB 23 '87			
MAR 16 '87			
GAYLORD			PRINTED IN U.S.A.